Working Smart

A Blueprint for Success in the Corporate Workplace

Dr. Addons Wu

Dear Todd,

Best Regards!

Addons

9/25/14

Copyright © 2014
All rights reserved.
ISBN-13: 978-0692236598

To my children

Contents

Preface ix

1 Blueprint for Success 17

2 Developing a Professional Attitude 23
    2.1   Uphold a Professional Attitude 23
    2.2   Act Out the Role 28
    2.3   Be Humble 30
    2.4   Be Fearless 32
    2.5   Think Bigger 33
    2.6   Know Your Priorities 35
    2.7   Stop Doing What is Unimportant 36

3 Preparing for Opportunities 41
    3.1   Plan a Career Path 41
    3.2   Do Your Best in Your Current Job 48
    3.3   Be Prepared for Opportunities 51
    3.4   Invest in Your Future 55
    3.5   Increase Your Value 59
    3.6   Avoid Becoming Obsolete 62
    3.7   Strike a Balance 63

4 Adapting to Workforce Dynamics 71
    4.1   Mark Your Presence 71
    4.2   Be Alert of Potential Dangers 76
    4.3   Be a Squeaky Wheel 78
    4.4   Avoid Being a High Maintenance Employee 79
    4.5   Enjoy Making Changes 80
    4.6   Safeguard Your Reputation 81
    4.7   Develop Self-awareness 83
    4.8   Benefit from a Mentor 84
    4.9   Communicate to Reinforce Your Professional Image .. 88
    4.10 Strike a Balance 91

5 Connecting with Your Boss 101

- 5.1 Be Loyal to Your Boss 101
- 5.2 Frame the Perception 104
- 5.3 Promote Your Visibility 108
- 5.4 Do Not Shoot Yourself in the Foot 112
- 5.5 Connect with Bad Bosses 116
- 5.6 Package Your Message 120
- 5.7 Communicate with a Purpose 120
- 5.8 Strike a Balance 126

6 Influencing Your Peers 135

- 6.1 Understand Your Peers' Objectives 136
- 6.2 Keep Your Peers Closer 138
- 6.3 Anticipate Surprises 141
- 6.4 Never Talk Negatively About Your Teammates 141
- 6.5 Communicate to Win 143
- 6.6 Strike a Balance 145

7 Leading Your Subordinates 153

- 7.1 Be a Leader 153
- 7.2 Be a Coach 155
- 7.3 Treat Employees with Respect 161
- 7.4 Develop People 166
- 7.5 Build and Sustain a High Performance Team 169
- 7.6 Establish an Organizational Culture 175
- 7.7 Institute a Fun Work Environment 177
- 7.8 Put Your Employees at the Right Post 181
- 7.9 Connect with Low Performers 183
- 7.10 Establish Your Own Ambassadors 187
- 7.11 Communicate to Get Alignment 189
- 7.12 Strike a Balance 192

8 Your Search for Success 201

- 8.1 Define Your Own Success 201
- 8.2 Follow Your Heart 205
- 8.3 Practice What You Learned 208

Preface

I sincerely hope this book will benefit you – the hard working and driven individuals of the corporate workforce who want to contribute more to your organizations and advance your careers.

This book will show you how to work smart, but more importantly, it aims to lead you toward a more satisfying and joyful life. By becoming more effective at work, you also increase your ability to connect with your family and devote energy to what is most important to you.

In my more than thirty-five years of professional experience, which includes long-term work assignments across five countries in North America, Europe, and Asia, I have come across many intelligent and determined individuals who start with lofty career goals but then fall short of achieving them. In a majority of cases, the underlying weaknesses that hinder career advancement are not in "hard" technical skills. Rather, it stems from weaknesses in "soft" professional skills such as:

- Displaying a professional attitude
- Seizing and creating opportunities
- Adapting to workplace dynamics
- Connecting with peers and bosses
- Communicating effectively

Throughout my career, I have prioritized the development of my employees. It is a responsibility I enjoy very much and am deeply passionate about. I work closely with each individual to clarify, set, and realize their career goals through tailored feedback and guidance. This book allows me to share with a wider audience my observations, experiences, and insights to achieving success.

I am fortunate to have led teams of varying sizes and composition, across different industries and geographies. In this book I draw from these experiences:

a) I have worked for extended periods in the UK, Canada, the US, South Korea, and China. Each country has its own unique culture and work style. For example, working in a team of all Europeans is very different from working in a team of all Chinese. Along the same lines, leading a group of South Korean employees is very different from leading a group of American employees. The global trend is accelerating towards diverse teams composed of multiple nationalities.

b) I have led teams of employees representing different educational levels and socio-economic backgrounds. My experience spans a variety of industries such as information technology, automobile, building material, business consulting, education, and manufacturing. When working in the information technology industry, I was surrounded by highly educated professionals. In the automobile industry, I had the opportunity to interact with factory workers, and to be led by leaders who had spent the majority of their careers managing blue collar employees. The style and philosophy of management that is effective for one organization may not be most effective for another.

c) I have led teams ranging from large to small. At one extreme, I have held executive management roles overseeing large scope of responsibility but with no direct reports.

d) I have worked in highly structured environments that adhere strictly to eight-hour work days and where objectives and deliverables are well defined. I also have worked in highly dynamic "battlefield" situations, which were entrepreneurial and fast-paced. In one "battlefield" situation, I was sent by my company to China to create new business opportunities and expand business operations.

e) I have worked in multinational corporations that operate within a set of comprehensive business processes. I also have worked in smaller companies that are much less process-oriented, where agreements and business decisions are made primarily through relationships and informal negotiations among key stakeholders.

f) I have worked for many great leaders and benefited immensely from observing their differing styles of leadership. Naturally, I also worked with difficult leaders in my career, and even some that were eager to eliminate me from their teams.

g) I have been working as an expatriate in China for more than fifteen years. Through this experience, I developed a thorough understanding of Chinese workforce dynamics, and the leadership styles that are uniquely effective in China.

Each time I transitioned to a new leadership position, it was imperative that I accurately assess the situation and adapt my work style accordingly to match the needs of the organization. Unavoidably, there have been cases where I did not adjust quickly enough.

I recall moments where I thought I had made all the right decisions and done all the right things, only to discover that I was completely wrong. On several occasions, I was at the brink of losing my job due to mistakes of my own or inappropriate actions committed by my team. And of course there were the inevitable situations where I had to deal with politically motivated colleagues, those who achieve success by stepping on other people and behaving without integrity. To protect my team and myself, I had to focus on anticipating what could go wrong and taking appropriate countermeasures.

I also had my share of luck and successes. In my early career, I promptly seized opportunities that came my way and worked hard at proactively creating new ones.

When I was thirty-eight, I was awarded "Best Manager" and "Excellence in People Development" from my department. When I was forty-one, I became the General Director of a leading global research and development organization. In the same year, I was awarded the most prestigious "Manager of the Year" title from my company, a multi-billion dollar revenue multinational corporation. When I was forty-four, I became one of the top 300 senior executives of the largest US corporation, which had revenues of more than $200B globally.

China is a market well known for being difficult to manage talent due to a rapidly growing economy. In fact, attracting talent, developing talent, and managing employee attrition are frequently cited as the top challenges of doing business in China. Contrary to industry norms, I have been particularly successful at building high performing teams and developing managerial talent in the country. The teams I grew and maintained were exceptionally stable, and their loyalty propelled my company's local business growth in China as well as contributed to global initiatives.

My professional career now spans more than thirty-five years. Reflecting upon my journey, I have worked through crises, I have seized opportunities, I have celebrated many successes, and I have learned from many of my mistakes. And I can humbly say that I survived.

In the larger scheme of our lives, I believe success requires balancing family, work, and our personal fulfillment.

In 2013, I published a book titled *Kids Come Second – And Other Unconventional Wisdom on Raising Great Children*. In that book, I shared my thoughts on being responsible to our families, raising our children, and putting our spouses first. I talked briefly about the importance of one's attitude toward work and life. I outlined a few methods that parents can follow to coach young children and develop their potential.

This book is about being successful in the workplace. I chose not to focus on leadership and management theories as these are not exact sciences. I also do not discuss survival skills in the workplace for similar reasons. The workplace holds an infinite number of possibilities, and issues often are not clearly black or white. Each situation depends on the business and the people involved – bosses, peers, and subordinates. Hence, no single theory can apply to all cases. Furthermore, leadership styles and survival skills are most effective when authentic, i.e. matched to a person's personality.

This book is intended to be a reference rather than a teaching tool. Through the blueprint and experiences that I share, my intention is that you will be able to examine your own situations in a different light, take action where appropriate, and achieve your career goals.

Before I began writing this book, I asked many colleagues and friends what topics within the realm of management and corporate workplace efficiency would spark their interest.

When reviewing all the responses, I found two recurring topics of interest.

1. How to become smarter and more successful in the workplace.
2. How to plan a career and how to get a job promotion.

In this book, I address these two topics, but have also taken a broader approach through the Blueprint for Success.

1
Blueprint for Success

Throughout my career, I have searched for a systematic approach to developing talent in the corporate workplace. I am convinced there is no step-by-step recipe to achieving success – I do not believe there are specific instructions we can give individuals, that when followed sequentially, will guarantee their growth and maturity.

I do strongly believe in the popular saying that describes how people are better rewarded, and hence more successful, if they show up at the right place, at the right time, and with the right people supporting them.

Working smart is about creating this favorable situation for yourself. You want this to occur more frequently to you than to others. You need to actively cultivate these favorable situations, instead of waiting for luck to come.

This is the basis for the Blueprint for Success I developed for achieving success in the corporate workplace. It centers on the concept of being present at the right place, at the right time, and with support from the right people. The Blueprint for Success is depicted in the diagram below:

Figure 1: Blueprint for Success in the corporate workplace.

The Blueprint for Success contains four components:

1. Developing a professional attitude: Nurturing the right professional attitude is the foundation to success in the corporate workplace. The other three components build on top of this.

2. Preparing for opportunities: Get ready to seize opportunities when they come your way. The right time can happen at any moment, when you least expect it.

3. Adapting to workplace dynamics: Increase the odds that you are at the right place at the right time. Increase the chances that decision makers think of you when opportunities arise.

4. Building connections: Surround yourself with the right people you can count on, and actively maintain these connections. Connect with your bosses, influence your peers, and lead your subordinates.

In this book, I devote one chapter to each of the components in the Blueprint for Success, except for Building connections which is covered by three chapters.

Achieving success in the workplace is a noble pursuit that should be carried out with both humility and dedication. The Blueprint for Success does not dictate a sequence of actions you must follow step-by-step. Instead, there are four distinct components that must be developed in parallel, which when combined, propels you toward success.

How much effort should you spend on developing your career? That very much depends on your definition of success. You are the only one that can decide what matters to you most and what brings you happiness. I devote the last chapter to exploring this topic with you.

"Humility is a foundation of all other virtues."
Confucius.

2

Developing a Professional Attitude

If you want to be successful, you must work hard.

2.1 Uphold a Professional Attitude

I would like to start with a couple of examples where employees gradually lost their passion and professional attitude over time.

I once knew an IT professional who was an expert in computing systems. She graduated from a prestigious university in computer science with high academic achievements. She was intelligent, cheerful, and a fast learner. After she graduated, she joined a company as an IT engineer and she worked there for ten years without changing jobs. Staying in one company has merits and is not necessarily a bad thing. Unfortunately, the company did not have challenging work to develop and make the full use of her talent. Worse yet, her manager did not develop her skills and did not demand high performance from her.

For the ten years working in the group, she was doing routine IT operations work. She did not see any reward when she put in extra effort to get her job done. Gradually, she became content with her situation and developed a relaxed attitude. She lacked a sense of urgency. She chose to do work that she found interesting instead of work that was important or urgent. She lost the drive to become a high achiever. She lost the professional attitude that was important in the golden years of her career journey.

Another example is about a person who was the IT leader at a remote facility of the company I used to work for. The remote facility had about one hundred employees. This IT leader and his subordinates supported the business with no major issues. However, there had been complaints regarding his responsiveness. Even though he didn't appear busy, he was slow in responding to phone calls and emails. When I discussed his poor response to customer calls, he gave me plenty of excuses of why he was slow, with little improvement following our discussions.

One summer, he told me that he would take a three-week vacation in Singapore and would not take his company PC with him. That meant that he would be out of touch for three weeks in Singapore, where Internet service was ubiquitous and connecting back to the company was quick and easy. From this incident, I judged that he was not dependable and he had lost the fundamental professional attitude to perform his job. And, I believed that he had accepted his behavior as a reasonable one.

Many people would say that passion is the most important factor to success since without passion people tend to pay less attention to their jobs. They tend to make more mistakes, and their job performance is less predictable. Therefore a minimal level of passion and an essential amount of professional attitude is required for people to survive in the workplace whether they treat their jobs as their first priority or not.

In the examples above, both employees displayed little passion in their jobs. They portrayed an unprofessional attitude for so long that their attitude became a habit. They were unaware that their inappropriate attitude was their problem and, thus, it was unlikely that they would improve their attitude. They may also be unaware that due to their poor attitude, their jobs had become vulnerable and their existence had become dispensable to their employers.

The examples above also paint a typical profile of employees who are skillful at their jobs but are never rewarded with any job promotions.

I always choose employees who display the right professional attitude over those who have the right technical skills. Once employees with the right professional attitude are trained, they always deliver better solutions that are in line with upholding company values. It is much easier to train someone technical skills than professional attitude.

An employee with a good professional attitude inspires others, communicates effectively, and models the right behavior.

Professional attitude is all about having the right and positive attitude toward work, such as:

- Adhering to all applicable laws and policies
- Being punctual, thus, respecting the valuable time of others
- Helping to maintain a safe workplace
- Demanding the best performance from oneself and in others
- Shouldering responsibilities
- Saying what needs to be said in an honest and respectful way
- Protecting the private and public environment from hazardous materials
- Complying with operating procedures and using the right tools
- Acting in a manner that upholds the organizational culture and image
- Demonstrating high integrity and good work ethics

Upholding a good professional attitude is important as many leaders have said, "Anyone can get a job done. What makes employees more outstanding is how they deliver their jobs, which are driven from their attitude."

It is interesting that some employees would do whatever it takes to deliver their jobs and more, while some others would contribute merely 80% of their efforts and claim that life is hard. And, some leaders would innovate and lead with a vision to take their team performance to higher plateaus, while some others would simply do the minimum and spend no effort to improve the status quo. The difference is in people's attitude.

Annual or quarterly employee performance assessment reviews are common place. In these, employees are assessed on their job achievements and personal skill development based on pre-established goals. The assessment rating could range between "Exceeding expectations", "Meeting expectations", and "Unacceptable performance".

Assessing an employee's job performance is typically a subjective judgment from the manager. That is, an employee who has completed all the goals could simply be rated as "Meeting expectations", and an employee who has failed to deliver all the goals could be rated as "Exceeding expectations". The difference of assessment is largely determined by how the goals are set and the employee's professional attitude toward their jobs.

I have always told my subordinates that employees are often promoted not because they are more knowledgeable or more skilled than others. They are often promoted because they have the right professional attitude.

2.2 Act Out the Role

A poem written by William Shakespeare begins with, "All the world's a stage, and all the men and women merely players." I believe that work is just like a play. When I act out my role, my judgments at work become more accurate and my actions become more impactful.

Occasionally, my staff would ask what professional attitudes and behaviors I value and they would strengthen those attitudes and behaviors accordingly. In practice, it is not easy to decipher your bosses' professional styles and match their styles.

I have one example to illustrate this point. One of my colleagues was very muscular. He lifted weights to keep fit. From his appearance, he was strong-minded and decisive. My boss assigned him important projects to manage. One winter, my company had to downsize our staff force to reduce operating costs. In a meeting that involved only the three of us, my boss asked my colleague and me to remove two employees from each of our teams. Surprisingly, my colleague who otherwise looked strong burst into tears. He found it emotionally difficult to terminate employment of two team members only for the sole reason of company financial struggles.

Two months later, my boss asked me to take over one of my colleague's projects. My boss' reason was that my colleague was emotionally weak because he cried. From this incident, I was surprised to know the true self of my colleague. I was also surprised about my boss' strong reaction to my colleague's emotional expression. Given a different boss, my colleague would have been treated differently.

There are a few interesting tidbits about me in the workplace:

- I maintain a perfectly clean desk at work while my work room at home is messy.
- I force myself to socialize with my colleagues at work while I enjoy being alone listening to music at home.
- I am decisive and serious at work while I am indecisive and playful at home.
- I am compliant to company guidelines and policies at work while I am flexible when interacting with families and friends.
- I am ruthless when needed at work while I am always kind with my families and friends.

A few of my subordinates used to tell me that for many years they always saw me with a serious, straight face. I seldom smiled. The reason was clear: I was acting out my role as I believed the job required.

One of my previous colleagues and I worked together for eight years in the same company. After I had left the company, he and I became good friends. We learned more about each other's personal character and value systems. Not surprisingly, he told me one day, "You are a different person than the one I used to know at work. You hide your personality very well!" My response to him in a semi-joking way was, "Indeed, if I did not act out my role at work, I would have been fired by the company many times over."

2.3   Be Humble

If there is only one characteristic that distinguishes a great person from a good one, humility.

In the workplace, an employee with a high degree of humility is a person who is humble yet maintains pride and dignity, who is not timid yet is not arrogant, and who respects other people.

Humility is the foundation for people to seek to understand others, to appreciate cultural differences, and to maintain an open mind and curiosity to alternatives, thus, opening up a window of higher achievements.

In short, humility is a foundation for building relationships.

Occasionally, I use the tactic of self-criticism to maintain a continuous dialogue with my colleagues. For example, whenever appropriate, I begin an email with a self-criticism such as, "Yesterday, I forgot to tell you that a decision was needed to be made this morning, I apologize." Although I use the word apologize, I say it in confidence and do not lose my dignity. In this case, being humble allows me to set up the right tone for the follow-on conversation.

There is a well-known Chinese wisdom that depicts humility very well, "In a group of three, there must be at least one person who can be my teacher." I have found that the more people have accomplished and the more confidence they have in themselves, the more humble they become. Humility is a source of energy for people to ask for help. Many times, people make mistakes because they are overly confident and do not realize that they are ignorant about all the possibilities.

I believe that humility is a virtue that can be learned. Humility is accumulated gradually through learning from the behaviors modeled by our parents, the ethical beliefs conveyed by our teachers, and the social norms exhibited by our friends and relatives. Humility is a reflection of who we are as a person.

I once tried to coach one of my subordinates to be humble. I coached and observed him for one year. As I expected, his progress was slow and gradual. The reason was that, fundamentally, he could not appreciate fully what humility meant in practical terms. He tried to be humble, but his actions reflected that he was not. Deep in his mind he believed that a few of his colleagues were incompetent. He ignored them instead of seeking to understand and learn from them. He had too much pride in himself to realize his own deficiencies. He struggled to build relationships with a few of his peers because fundamentally he did not respect them. He was too confident and occasionally failed to realize the need to ask for help.

There was another employee who struggled to realize that her lack of humility had prohibited her progress and negatively impacted her job performance. Many times, she either missed opportunities to ask or intentionally did not ask for help from others. As a result, her vision was narrow compared to other employees. Her judgments were blurred by her over-confidence in herself.

For me, humility is one of many attributes to my success. Due to the way I was raised in my childhood, humility is a part of me. I tend to think of myself less, which allows me to be more receptive to ideas, leads me to deal with situations assertively instead of aggressively, improves my relationships across all levels at work, reassures my self-confidence, and opens a window for me to achieve more.

2.4   Be Fearless

If you have no fear of losing your job, you would have a better chance of:

- Making more objective decisions
- Speaking more candidly to your bosses and peers
- Upholding your integrity – acting for the benefits of the company rather than for protecting your job security

My leadership behavior and professional attitude have evolved over time.

When I was a young professional, I was confident and fearless. I had my best job performances although I made mistakes.

Later in my career, as I had learned from my mistakes, I became more assertive, people-oriented, and more focused on larger company goals. I was extremely effective in prioritizing my work. However, I was also very cautious about protecting my job. In a way, I did not perform at my best potential.

Now, as I am reaching retirement age, I am at my best in terms of career performance as I have no worry about job security and I am, again, fearless.

2.5 Think Bigger

We need to force ourselves to be outside the confinement of our area of responsibilities in order to see the bigger picture and to make the right decision.

I was once asked to develop a strategy for the business unit I was leading. The unit had failed to achieve its business goals and had been a financial burden to the company for two consecutive years. The strategy to be developed and if accepted would dictate a major future step of the business unit.

As an integral part of the strategy, I explored all possible alternatives that would make the unit profitable as quickly as possible. I revised the vision to be more inspirational, established new tactics to win, and defined a new set of capabilities that was critical for the unit to succeed.

I submitted the strategy but to my disappointment it was rejected by my boss. I then revised the strategy and resubmitted it. And again, it was rejected. After two failures, my boss explained to me that my vision was too narrow. As the leader of the business unit, I was too emotionally attached to the unit resulting in me failing to see the bigger picture and the best strategy for the company. If I had focused on the bigger picture, it would have been obvious to me that the right strategy for the company was to shut down the business unit.

"I will behave like a general manager," said a previous colleague of mine. He included this as one of his goals for personal development, although he did not know what behaving like a general manager meant exactly. His boss did not know how to measure the progress associated with it either. However, since the goal in itself sounded great, my colleague and his boss were aligned with the goal, anticipating that it would drive a positive change in my colleague's leadership skills and professional attitude.

My colleague did the right thing in creating that goal.

At a minimum, behaving like a general manager meant that he needed to consider the bigger company profit goal when spending his departmental budget, he needed to consider the bigger talent implications to the company when he hired employees for his own department, he needed to be more curious about why things happened around the company, and he needed to consider the ultimate impacts to the company when deciding on whether a particular action was taken. As a result, his impact and influence pervaded areas beyond his immediate areas of responsibilities.

2.6   Know Your Priorities

It is interesting that not everyone knows his or her priorities although it takes only common sense to decide what is important or urgent.

I once had an important meeting with a sales director of a reputable vendor. During the first fifteen minutes of the meeting, the sales director's mobile phone rang twice and in both times after uttering the words, "Excuse me," she answered the phone for a couple of minutes, making everyone in the meeting to wait. Observing her inappropriate behavior, I sent a strong message to her by cancelling the meeting after she finished answering her second phone call.

"The sales director was impolite to her customer and did not know her priorities," you would say. I have seen many similar situations where people gave the wrong priority to the meetings they were attending – they let their phone calls to interrupt their meetings, paying little respect to those they were meeting with.

There are many criteria for determining priorities such as importance and urgency. However, despite how easy and logical it may seem, some people do have problems setting priorities, simply because they prioritize work that they enjoy doing, or that are easy to get done. For me, what has proven effective is that I always treat it as a priority to remove myself from the bottleneck of actions, that is, I prioritize the tasks that trigger further actions from others, or that are on critical paths of projects.

2.7 Stop Doing What is Unimportant

One aspect of working smart is to stop doing what provides little value, so that you free up time to do things that are of higher impacts to your company and personal growth.

Are you doing anything at work that is unimportant or that is of little value?

Perhaps, you stop reading this book for a while and think about what you can stop doing at work before reading on again.

Developing a Professional Attitude

Summary of key points:

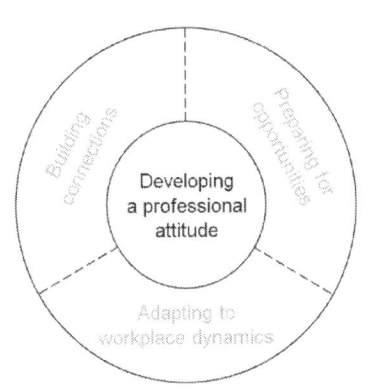

1. Don't lose the drive to become a high achiever. If you want to be successful, you must work hard. (Page 23)

2. Professional attitude is all about having the right and positive attitude toward work. An employee with a good professional attitude models the right behavior and inspires others. (Page 26)

3. Anyone can get a job done. What makes employees more outstanding is how they deliver their jobs, which are driven from their attitude. (Page 26)

4. Be humble. Think of yourself less, which allows you to be more receptive to ideas, leads you to deal with situations assertively instead of aggressively, improves your relationships across all levels at work, and opens a window for you to achieve more. (Page 30)

5. You will perform at your best if you are not fear about losing your job. (Page 32)

6. Look from the outside-in. Force yourself to be outside the confinement of your area of responsibilities in order to see the bigger picture and to make the right decision. (Page 33)

7. Remove yourself from the bottleneck of actions, that is, prioritize the tasks that trigger further actions from others, or that are on critical paths of projects. (Page 36)

8. Stop doing what provides little value so that you free up time to do things that are of higher impacts to your company and personal growth. (Page 36)

Success requires hard work.

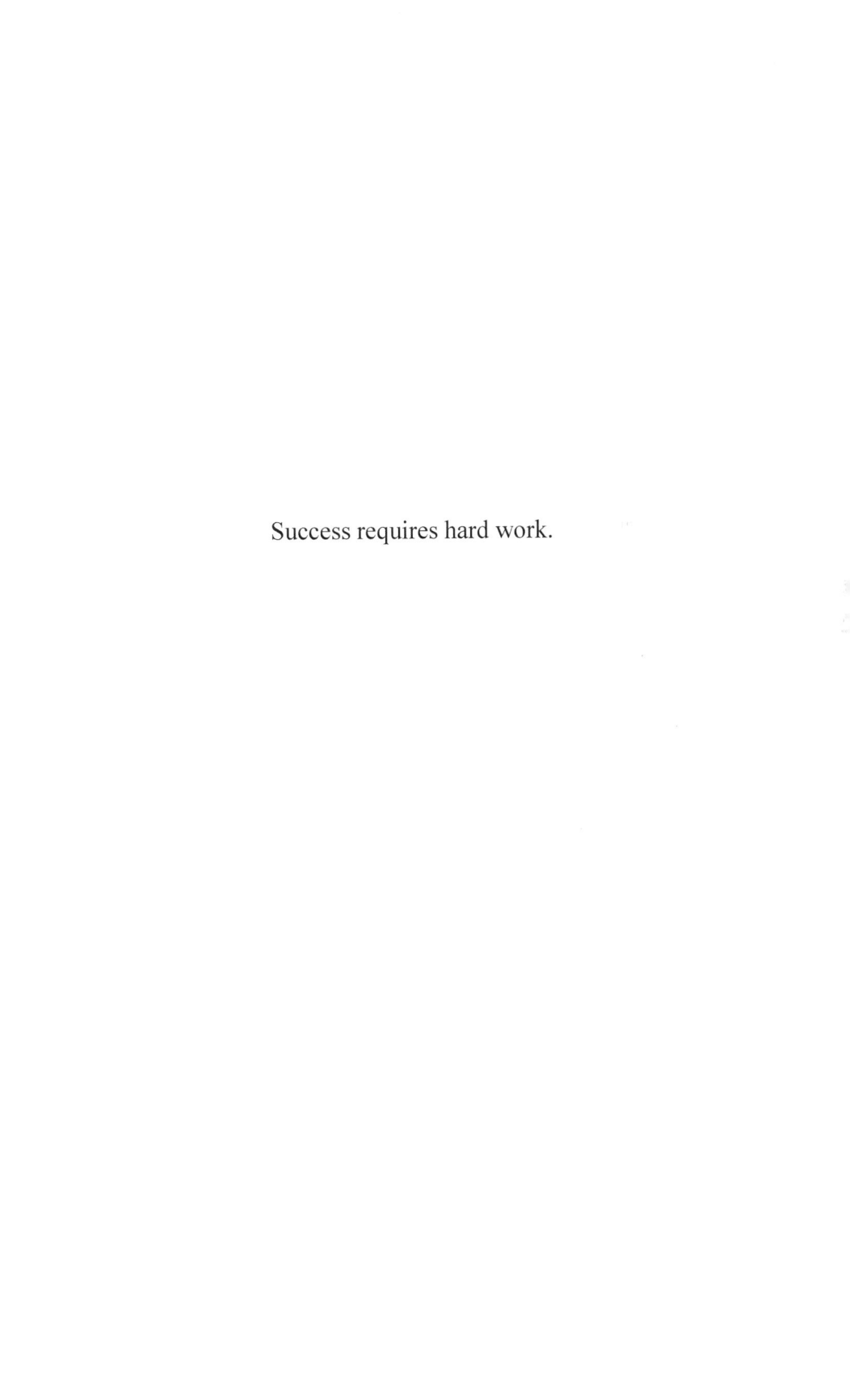

3

Preparing for Opportunities

3.1   Plan a Career Path

"Is your job your first priority in life?"

This is the first question I often throw back to my colleagues and subordinates when they asked me about career planning. This question typically directs the follow-on conversation into the right context.

If your job were the top priority in your life, you would be more concerned about your career path, and be more focused on your promotion possibilities and money earning power; your action will be more aggressive in achieving career goals and making preparations for opportunities to come.

On the other hand, if your career is not your top priority, you should focus your attention on where other passions lie. Practically, it is very difficult to place your career at a low priority and still progress, since you have to maintain an essential level of energy, enthusiasm, and professional attitude at work.

I always make time to interview and select candidates before allowing them to join my team, whether they report to me directly or not. During job interviews, I always ask candidates the following question:

"Where do you see yourself in five years and in ten years?"

Their answer tells me whether the candidates' career aspirations match the opportunities my company has to offer. It also gives me an idea of the candidates' attitude toward work. Both will allow me to mentally map out career paths and development plans of the candidates and form a judgment of their loyalty before they join the company. This tactic has been one of my secrets in building strong stable teams.

A clear career goal is the first fundamental decision before planning a career path. Of all the people with whom I have worked, I can broad-brush their career goals into the following categories:

- Seeking professional status
- Gaining experience
- Pursuing interest
- Climbing the corporate ladder
- Securing a stable income

If your career goal is to seek a good professional status you must focus on a path that strengthens your professional skills and enhances your technical knowledge. Any divergence from this goal is a distraction. For example, to accomplish career goals such as becoming a chief designer of a software company, a legal counsel of a large corporation, a chief architect of a construction company, or a surgical doctor requires strong foundations and continuous enhancements of professional experience and technical knowledge.

Many fresh university graduates have a simple career goal in mind. All they want is to acquire working experience. In fact, although this goal seems simple, it is not a bad goal for young energetic people who are still searching for their career interests. With the goal of gaining experience in mind, you must plan a career path that provides the most classroom training and on-the-job learning opportunities. This means that changing jobs or changing companies to gain a wide spectrum of experience may become an integral part of your career path. In today's work environment, having experience from multiple companies during your early career, whilst maintaining your sense of loyalty, is a good career strategy. For example, changing companies once every three years during the first ten years of your career is a good career path.

If your career goal is all about pursuing your personal interests, then job status is less important. I have known a few friends whose sole interests are in educating the younger generations; there is no lack of people who are focused on seeking their ideals of serving the community; there are people whose career goals are simply to enjoy coming to work every day while prioritizing their family; there are people who enjoy working alone on a computer; and there are people who devote their whole life to carrying out scientific research. These are all successful people.

I have come to realize that the majority of people I know have a goal of climbing the corporate ladder whether propelled by their own desire of making more money, building stronger self-esteem, or simply being competitive. I have seen many talented, energetic people who became "successful" simply because they have this goal in mind. I put "successful" in quotes because I believe that money and job status are merely two of many aspects of success. There are many other important considerations in a person's life. The career path to achieve the goal of climbing the corporate ladder may take many different forms.

Of course, some people are content with a stable job that generates stable income as their career goal.

It is natural that as a person matures, their career goal changes. Take myself as an example: I personally have had different goals in different stages of my career. After I graduated from school and started working, my career goal was simply to pursue my personal interests. As time passed, my career goal has evolved from pursuing interests, to gaining experience, to seeking professional status, and finally I am back to pursuing interests.

Being flexible and being able to quickly adapt to job market demands are important when executing career plans.

A career path is greatly influenced by many external factors. Maintaining a balance of short-term gains and long-term goals is important. For example, there have been many success stories of people who changed their jobs not following their original career plans and became very happy and successful. They did it either by choice or by coincidence, often because of a promotion or an increase in salary. On the other hand, I have also seen people who failed after choosing to change their career.

In 2009, I listened to a speech made by the president of a large US based global company. She intentionally made the following point in exaggeration: "A career cannot be planned." Her point was that career paths of many successful employees are sometimes crafted by the senior leadership team based on their observation and judgment of the employees' professional strengths.

In the companies I have worked for, I have seen many situations where job assignments and opportunities were given to employees who were identified as potential future leaders of the company. These job assignments might not align with the assignees' career paths. The objectives of these assignments were to groom high potential employees to become future leaders. However, due to various reasons and company policies, the objectives of the assignments could not be clearly translated into promises of future promotions or career growth. Therefore, the purpose of the assignments might not be viewed as an advantage from the employees' perspective.

For example, I have seen high potential employees assigned smaller jobs, which appeared seemingly irrelevant to their career goals. However, shortly after the smaller job assignments, they were rewarded with big promotions. Also, I have known engineers who were asked to take a two-year expatriate assignment in a third-world country to develop global experiences. Upon completing the expatriate assignments, they were awarded with higher levels of responsibilities.

In my case, I was once given the opportunity to change my job from a software development manager to a hardware development team leader, responsible for circuit board design. I took the job even though I disliked hardware development and was concerned about the disruption of my career path.

My decision to take the hardware development job paid off. One year after the new assignment, I was promoted to a senior managerial position, leading product development, which comprised of both software and hardware development.

In hindsight, I was sure my manager asked me to take the hardware development job because he believed that I was a potential future leader of the company. If I had not accepted my company's arrangement to take the hardware development job, the promotion opportunity would have most probably been given to another person in the company.

Employees who show faith and loyalty to their company by doing what the company asks often come out ahead in their career advancements.

Referring back to my earlier example, the president's real advice was that if you wanted to climb the corporate ladder, you should seriously consider the assignment asked by the company even though the assignment did not appear to match your career interests.

Many success stories have proven that although careers might not work out as planned, the outcome can surprisingly be favorable. Many people became successful after they had changed their career either by coincidence or by choice. Sometimes, it really takes a drastic change to one's career path in order to understand where one's interest truly lies. When facing tough career path decisions, one may have to follow one's heart.

I remember many years ago my company sent a few junior managers as expatriate employees to China. Two colleagues of mine accepted the assignment then subsequently quit the company and set up their own corporations in China after a few years. Creating their own companies had never been in their career plans. They simply followed their hearts after they saw the opportunities. Two others accepted the expatriate assignment and also quit their jobs. They joined other companies in China. They successfully climbed the corporate ladder and became top corporate executives. They realized that their initial career goals were too small and narrow-minded.

To plan a career, a good approach is for us to develop a detailed career path so that when unexpected opportunities arise we are prepared to take full advantage of the opportunities.

I am frequently surprised by how little I know about my own capabilities and how vast possibilities are outside my realm of understanding. The better planning we have, the higher is our self-awareness and the better we are prepared to seize the rare opportunities and anticipate the sudden career turns that come our way.

3.2   Do Your Best in Your Current Job

"How do I get a job promotion?"

One of my subordinates once asked me what qualifications he would need to be equipped with before he could be promoted to the next level. I could answer his question in many ways. However, I gave him a short and firm answer. I skipped all the details and told him, "Work hard. Do your best in your current job!"

Companies always promote the most capable person of a team to become the next leader. The most capable person is one who is the best performer and has a high potential to be a future leader.

In over thirty-five years of work experience, I have found that high performing employees are consistently promoted. For example, a sales person with the highest sales revenue and sales techniques is often destined for promotion as the next leader; an accountant with the best analytical and communication skills is often offered more responsibilities; a highly competent and effective leader in manufacturing is an ideal candidate to take on the role of the chief operating officer of a company.

There is one common advice that mentors often give their mentees. The advice is that while doing the current job, you should learn skills and pick up knowledge required for your future dream job. You have to be very careful in following this advice because, practically, if you are not doing a good job already, focusing only on developing skills for the next level job would not give you better chances to be promoted.

The most effective way to prove that you have the aptitude and attitude to qualify for the next job is to do your current job well.

Let me share an analogy that I learned from one of my mentors. He said that work is like water. Work flows to the most competent person or organization until an equilibrium point is reached. This analogy is in perfect alignment with a Chinese proverb that says: "Competent people get the most work!" The more focus you put on doing your current job well, the more competent you become, the more work flows your way, and the more often you show up at the right time when opportunities present themselves for you to grow.

If you look around the workplace, you will find examples of competent people carrying multiple jobs and doing their work well. These are the people who will get the next job promotion opportunities. For example, I used to know a great leader who was the Chief Information Officer (CIO) of a company. Because of his strong leadership as a CIO, he was given the added responsibility to lead the global supply chain and human resources functions. Another example is about me. I worked extremely hard early in my career. Before I was promoted from an engineer to a manager, I had a job with broad responsibilities. After my promotion, my company had to hire two people to do my previous job as an engineer. Broad responsibilities helped me acquire broader skills, which in turn positioned me to be stronger than my peers for job promotions.

In a competitive and growing economy where opportunities are ample, people are often promoted to their highest level of competence and potentially then to a role in which they are not competent, referred to as their level of incompetence.

3.3 Be Prepared for Opportunities

"Success will come when preparation meets opportunities." John Hartman.

There are many things we must do in preparation for the next career advancement to come.

First, we must do our current job well.

Second, we must make ourselves available for the promotion or job assignments when opportunity knocks.

Making ourselves available applies especially to those people who have subordinates and are ready for internal advancements. Numerous times, I have seen employees blocked from an internal opportunity because no one could replace them in their existing jobs. Therefore, it is important that we have a successor ready so that we can be freed from the current job at any time.

Third, we must plan our future job assignments. We must know what skills our company needs and acquire those skills, regardless of whether it creates a temporary slow-down of our career path.

Let me use myself as an example. I used to work in a research and development company in the telecommunications industry. When I first joined the company, I was an IT professional responsible for developing software applications to improve employee productivity. One day, my friend advised me: "If you want to be valued by your company, you ought to work at the core of your company's products and services." He hinted that my career future was limited being an IT professional in a company specialized in telecommunications. He was right. So I asked my company to give me an internal transfer and switched my job from supporting internal employees to a product engineer responsible for developing software products for my company to sell. As a result, my value became more relevant to the business!

After a couple of years working as a product engineer, I found that my communication skills had restricted my job performance. Realizing this deficiency, I asked for another job transfer, to become a technical report writer. This change was a major disruption to my career, but the results paid off.

In my two years working as a technical report writer, I learned how to structure technical reports. I became skilled in organizing raw data into usable information and I improved my English communication skills in a magnitude that no other job could give me.

Two years later, after I moved back to work as a product engineer, my performance was deemed outstanding, mostly due to my strong improvement in communication skills. I was good at both developing products and in communicating with my peers and senior executives. In fact, the technical report writing skills I learned benefited me for the rest of my career.

I am often asked if a higher degree would enhance someone's career. My reaction was that if people could afford the financial investment and time commitment, a higher degree could certainly help their careers. There are three aspects to be considered:

- Knowledge
- Professional image
- Professional maturity

First, from the knowledge aspect, if a person qualifies for the minimum educational requirements of a job, a higher degree does not make a person more qualified.

Second, higher degrees such as a Masters in Business Administration (MBA) or a Masters in Finance can certainly makes one's resume more impressive. The impact of these additional qualifications can be felt when a person is considered for job promotions within the same company or interviewed for jobs external to the company.

For example, I have a Doctorate degree (Ph.D.) in Computer Science. Although I never had the opportunity to use the subject knowledge I gained from this degree in my career, it helped me successfully apply for new jobs. When interviewers found I had a Ph.D. degree, they automatically, and correctly, assumed that I possess a minimum level of intelligence and ability.

Last, pursuing a higher degree is one way to enhance people's professional maturity. For example, through pursuing an

MBA degree, people can build personal connections with their classmates who are from different companies and industries and are of different cultural backgrounds. Through pursuing a higher degree, people naturally broaden their visions, become more conscious of global trends, and enrich their professional attitude and presence. It helps people perform better in their jobs.

A friend of mine did not graduate from university because she needed to take care of her family. She began her career as an accountant. Her company did not subsidize her for any skill training courses. Realizing the need to continue to improve herself, she paid for her own training classes to improve her negotiation skills and decision making skills. It is rare to see people pay for their own training in order to do their job better. It takes strong self-awareness and self-motivation to do what is right and necessary.

Last year, as I was strolling along Xintiandi in Shanghai, China, I saw posters that said, "Shanghai is soaring high! Where are you?" The message sent me into deep thoughts. Indeed, Shanghai is one of the centers of economic growth in China, and China has been growing fast for over twenty years and is continuing to grow fast. Where else do you want to be? I have the privilege to have worked in China and witnessed the fast economic growth there. The experience widens my vision of the global economy, global business operations, people development, and the meaning of life.

With the Chinese economy booming, it is definitely valuable for foreign workers, whether they are already seasoned professionals or just starting on their career journey, to seek experience in the Chinese market.

As the world becomes more globally connected, more companies value employees with work experiences in different ethnic groups and company cultures. Employees who have experiences working in multiple cities, countries, and companies are especially valued. These employees often provide different external perspectives, which fuel continuous improvements. Hence, seeking for diverse experiences is extremely worthwhile.

3.4   Invest in Your Future

An illusionist stood in front of a small bench on an otherwise empty stage, carrying nothing in his hands. He then waved a large black cloth in front of him and the bench. A few seconds later, he raised the cloth. Surprisingly, a fish bowl of approximately eight inches in diameter, filled with water and a goldfish appeared on the bench. The excitement from the audience was phenomenal. It was a great illusion.

The above show has made a lasting memory in my mind. I like magic shows. I have heard that magicians and illusionists plant their plots for many years before they actually perform the acts of illusion. This story tells how much preparation and sacrifice an illusionist makes to put up an exceptional performance.

How did the illusionist do the trick?

He did it by making a personal sacrifice for ten long years. The illusionist was thin, but for ten years before the act he dressed as a heavy-built person carrying a heavy load around his stomach beneath his clothes. He wore loosely fitted clothing to hide what he carried. He walked in a slow tempo. From his appearance, he was over-weight and was clumsily slow. No one was aware of what's hidden behind his superficial appearance.

On stage, he walked toward the bench carrying a huge fish bowl around his stomach that no one suspected. He walked in his normal slow pace to make sure that water did not spill from the fish bowl. At the bench, he was back to his nimble self. Hidden behind the black cloth, with a quick motion, he moved the fish bowl onto the bench.

We need to invest in our futures. Investments and sacrifices come in pairs and they take on many different forms. Fortunately, we do not need to experience the extreme sacrifices that the illusionist did in the story.

Where do we invest our time?

I always believe that time is not a problem. Despite the fact that time is limited, we always have time.

It is deciding on what to do, and not to do with our time that is important.

Do we spend more time on the job, thus sacrifice our time to enjoy life or to be with our family?

Jack Welch described the situation well, "There's no such thing as work-life balance. There are work-life choices, and you make them, and they have consequences."

I always insist on one principle and that is that people must work hard when they are still young. I have known young professionals, for example, dentists, who immediately upon graduation, seek to work four-day weeks. I am sure that if they worked harder to invest in their futures while they were young, their future success and contributions to society would have been greater.

In general, the higher up we are on the corporate ladder, the broader our job responsibilities and the more uncertain the situations we need to deal with. As a result, as we hold more senior jobs, we need to stay alert and react to emergencies beyond the normal eight-hour work day.

For example, I have been working as a Chief Information Officer (CIO) for more than fifteen years at three different global companies and industries. As a CIO, 10% of my job is to ensure that the business runs without unexpected interruptions. This means that I have to be aware of, and fix, any information network problems and computing system malfunctions on a round-the-clock basis. I will lose my job if I do not perform well in this 10% of my responsibilities.

I am sure everyone has his or her turn to be less busy at work. However, not everyone knows how to make the best use of his or her spare time at work. In fact, the more senior a job position, the more vague the job description. Many inexperienced people may find that they have more time to spare just because their job descriptions are vague and they do not know how or have not done enough to deliver their job objectives.

To me, having free time is a rare opportunity for me to invest in my future. I use my free time to explore if my job objectives can be expanded. I use my free time to interact with my peers to understand their work and to offer help as appropriately. Through these interactions, I expanded my vision and indirectly created a demand for my expertise. Consequently, I end up with no time to spare at all.

Many years ago, I witnessed one of my subordinates, who not only failed to make the best use of his spare time to invest in his future, but also let himself fall into a state of laziness. In his case, due to a change of business priorities, one of his projects was cancelled and he had about two hours to spare per day for six months. During that time, he did not treasure his spare time to do something innovative. Instead, he used his spare time to surf the Internet, text with his friends, and he left work early. He fell into a state of laziness from which it was hard for him to exit.

His failure to seize the opportunity to smartly invest his free time at work created a long-term detrimental impact on his career. Although he completed his job objectives, no more, no less, leaving work early became his habit. In addition, he unknowingly became addicted to diverting his attention to his mobile phone during work and at meetings, giving others the impression that he did not devote 100% of his time on work. The problem became so obvious that people noticed his improper behavior. As time passed, he gradually lost his impact on the organization along with his passion and self-esteem. Work assignments flowed away from him and his performance dropped to the bottom among his peers.

3.5 Increase Your Value

Occasionally, when my colleagues are promoted, I question: "Why not me?"

Maybe I did not have the right attitude.

Maybe the person who was promoted was stronger than me.

Maybe I underestimated what it took to be qualified for the next job, or simply that I lacked connections with my bosses and peers.

No matter what the reason, it boiled down to the fact that my existing skills did not match the job demand.

Many times, I have advised my subordinates not to despair if they don't get promoted. Instead, they should re-evaluate their skills against the industry demands and improve on their skills accordingly.

Asking for promotions too aggressively while lacking the skill-set may backfire on them as the business world is competitive. The higher the job position they hold, the more unforgiving their job performance. The higher up they climb the corporate ladder, the harder they fall when mistakes are made. I always tell them that a couple more years waiting for a promotion in the span of a 40-year work life is not significant. It is well worth the wait if two more years of waiting builds a more solid foundation of technical and professional skills.

The job market is governed by supply and demand. It is important that we understand how marketable our skills are so we do not become stagnant. Every job position has a market value. That means that within a certain job, a person's salary is determined based on the job position's market value, perhaps within a 20% deviation from the mean. To avoid becoming stagnant within a job, one has to continually upgrade one's skills to match the ever evolving job requirements.

For every job, there are two categories of skill requirements. Many people label these two categories as hard skills and soft skills.

Hard skills are referred to as technical knowledge and competencies specific to getting the job done, for example, compiling a consolidated financial statement, operating a stamping machine, designing business processes, analyzing business data, or cooking a gourmet dish. Hard skills are easy to measure and calibrate. They can be attained through on-the-job training.

Soft skills are also referred to as professional skills, but are harder to measure. In fact, the ability to learn new knowledge quickly is a soft skill. A person who is more equipped with soft skills is more promotable. Other examples of soft skills are curiosity and the ability to communicate. Soft skills accumulate over time and are portable from one job to another.

A friend of mine is an intelligent and hardworking individual who puts his career as his top priority. Many years ago, he told me that once every two years, he had discussions with job search firms about his career plans. He said that his objective was not to actively find a job, but to understand the job market and how his skills measured up against the job market demands. Through connecting with search firms, he changed his jobs numerous times. He had his moments of job successes and failures. When he failed, he climbed back up. Now, he is a senior vice president of a global company.

Talking to a search firm once every two years is not my style and I did not follow my friend's advice. However, certainly, within the context of understanding the job market, and learning to increase one's value in alignment with job market demands, job search firms do provide good insight and a source of information.

3.6 Avoid Becoming Obsolete

Surviving in the workplace is like rowing upstream in a river – if you don't row forward, you will be pushed backward.

The job market is constantly changing. For example, new job positions are frequently created due to the introduction of new products and services; companies are frequently forced out of business due to market competition and change of customer demands; and jobs are often eliminated due to technology advancements and process automation. As a result, job requirements are continually changing.

If we stay in the same job doing the same work for a long time there are many unfavorable consequences. First, as the job requirements change our skills become obsolete. Second, unless our jobs are of no significance to the organization, we block job advancements and skill development of other people and we will soon be moved aside so that others have room for growth.

The workplace is competitive in that we compete with our peers and new entrants to stay ahead. We have to distinguish ourselves from the rest to maintain a competitive edge by continuously improving our professional attitude and refreshing our skills. When we stop improving ourselves, we become irrelevant.

3.7 Strike a Balance

Being loyal to your own career versus to your employer

When I was in Canada, I worked for the most prestigious high technology company in the country. The company provided good salary, benefit packages, and stable jobs. For one year, the company had 100% of its job applicants accepting its job offers. For many people, it was a dream company to work for. However, one day, my colleague told me that he had just resigned and was planning to join a smaller company, where he was given higher responsibilities. It was hard for me to understand why he would quit the company, which everybody loved to join. He gave me one piece of advice that has benefited me for the rest of my career. He said, "Act like a hero! Do not change from a hero into a 'nobody' just because you like your company."

Being loyal to your company is a great professional attribute. However, unless you are truly content with the work environment, it is important that you do not forget about your own career goals.

Several situations warrant leaving your job or company.

For example:
- If you are not happy with the boss or the personality of the team, you should leave.
- If you find that the company does not make full use of your talent, you should leave.

- If you are capable and ambitious, you should look around for more opportunities.

If you are not happy with your current job, would you reduce your salary and forfeit your company benefits to leave your company to join a new one?

I have known a few friends who suffered through their jobs while they had the ability to leave. Leaving an unhappy job to seek a happier life is a personal choice and, sometimes, requires financial sacrifices and is a tough decision to be balanced.

For example, some years ago, one of my colleagues decided against making any job changes although he was not too happy with the nature of his job. He was an engineer but his job was routine and not challenging. He was bored. He asked me to help him find a new job in another company. In response to his request, I asked him a very basic question: "You need to think about whether you are really ready to give up your current stable job to explore something uncertain and new. If you are ready, talk to me again."

In the next seven years, he never initiated any actions to change his job. I believe that based on my question about his intent, he knew what he wanted. He wanted the stable high income job that he already had. Job challenge was secondary. To me, there is nothing wrong about not making a job change.

How about leaving a company that lacks business integrity?

I have been lucky that every company I have worked for had high business integrity. Therefore, I never had to make a decision of leaving a company that lacked business ethics. Despite how obvious the right decision is, it may be hard for a person to quit a company that does not act with integrity.

I came across one person during an interviewing session. He had applied for a financial accounting job in my company. During the interview, he told me that he had been out of work for three months. He left his previous company because he did not want to be associated with a company wrong doing that he discovered. I gave him my full respect based on his actions. On the contrary, I have known a couple of friends who had stayed with their companies which were of low business integrity, and found themselves tangled in law suits and had their careers and families ruined.

Developing your strengths versus improving your weaknesses

We should never stop improving ourselves!

There are two choices of self-improvement: we can develop our strengths or we can improve our weaknesses.

Within a certain period of time, we probably have time and energy to only focus on no more than three areas of improvements. Hence, it is important that we have a strong sense of self-awareness. I have found that many people automatically spend their energy on identifying their weaknesses and improving on them. Although it is not a mistake for people to focus their energy solely on improving their weaknesses, often, it makes much more sense for them to focus on developing their strengths and to become experts on certain skills and knowledge.

There are a couple of considerations when deciding which skills we improve or strengthen:

1. Our strengths, if we do not pay attention, could degrade to our blind spots or weaknesses.

2. Personal development is about becoming who we can be instead of changing who we are: Some personal characters are hard to change. For example, the most stressful or unnatural change could be for a quiet person to become actively vocal in group meetings. Developing skills that complement our personal characters is more effective than correcting them.

In general, I have found that employees who are inexperienced should be more focused on improving their weaknesses, and experienced and mature employees should be more focused on further strengthening their fortes.

Preparing for Opportunities

Summary of key points:

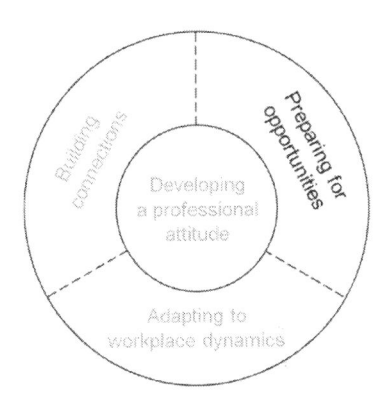

1. You will come out ahead in your career advancements if you show faith and loyalty to your company by doing what your company asks. (Page 45)

2. The better career planning you have, the higher is your self-awareness and the better you are prepared to seize the rare opportunities and anticipate the sudden career turns that come your way. (Page 48)

3. The best way to get a promotion is to do your best in your current job. (Page 48)

4. It is important that you have a successor ready so that you can be freed from the current job at any time. (Page 51)

5. A higher educational qualification enhances your professional knowledge, broadens your vision, and improves your professional maturity. Obtain a higher degree if you can afford the financial investment and time commitment. (Page 53)

6. If it fits your personal agenda, getting diverse work experiences from an international assignment is extremely worthwhile. (Page 54)

7. Invest your free time at work to develop yourself. Once you slip into a state of laziness, it is extremely hard to exit from it. (Page 58)

8. Upgrade your skills continuously to match the ever evolving job requirements to avoid becoming stagnant or irrelevant. (Page 60)

9. Personal development is about becoming who you can be instead of changing who you are. (Page 65)

When there are people involved, simple situations may become complex or unpredictable.

4

Adapting to Workforce Dynamics

4.1 Mark Your Presence

In the corporate workplace, if you are not visible to others in a positive way, you will be ignored and forgotten, and your existence will become insignificant. As a result, no opportunity or luck will fall on you. I have been strongly motivated by a quote from Brian Tracy, "I've found that luck is quite predictable. If you want more luck, take more chances, be more active, show up more often."

During my career, I have tried numerous tactics to mark my presence in different situations in order to gain the mindshare of other people. For example, when I visited another company location on a business trip, I seldom ate meals alone. I always ate lunch and dinner with my business colleagues. Meals do not need to be luxurious. There have been numerous dinner occasions when I enjoyed a bowl of noodles from a Thai restaurant with my colleagues.

While visiting other locations, I also made appointments to have one-on-one discussions with leaders who held more senior positions, even though I never had any prior business engagements with them. My agenda for these one-on-one discussions was simple: I provided a brief update of what I was doing and I listened to the leaders about what they could share with me about the company. I seldom prepared for these discussions except that, occasionally, I brought a presentation slide with me. I found that senior leaders always have something in their mind to talk about: they always liked to share their experiences and insights and, occasionally, they were quick to point out my mistakes.

Many people are awarded for their achievements and successes because they are present at the right place at the right time.

In order to increase the chances to be around at the right place at the right time, people really need to make an effort to be around all the time.

For example, when I was a young professional, I joined a couple of company initiatives that were of long-term significance: I was in a recruiting team for two years to interview and hire fresh graduates from universities to join our company; I was in a team of instructors of an internal leadership development program; and I taught a course on "building customer relationships".

I once knew a colleague who always carried a book in his hand when he came to work. Another colleague of mine pursued a Ph.D. degree in his spare time at the age of forty-five. Many friends I knew actively organized and participated in company social events. And, many others made the effort to have lunch with their colleagues instead of eating alone. All these efforts helped to mark their presence in others' minds.

I have told the following story to my children a couple of times.

One day, I was on a business trip to visit another company site. I was in the office around 7:30 in the morning. Since I was only visiting, I did not have my own office and I sat by myself in an empty conference room. My plan was to print an important document for a meeting, which was scheduled to start at 8:00am. I needed to find a printer and I needed to configure my PC to print the document. I walked around the office and I found a printer. I saw no one in the office. I returned to the conference room and tried to configure my PC to connect to the printer. An employee, whom I knew from the human resources (HR) department, walked into the conference room and asked if I needed help. As I had not seen anybody earlier, he must have seen me from his own work area afar. Since he was from the HR department, I did not expect that he could help to configure my PC. Nonetheless, I told him what I needed and to my surprise, he quickly set up my PC for printing. He saved me time and freed me from anxiety. I was impressed by this colleague's attitude and keenness to help me.

A couple of months later, I was in a committee to review employee performances of a few departments. Among the employees to be reviewed was the person who had helped me earlier with printing. I seized the opportunity to emphasize his professional attitude. I also found that his attitude was also felt by other leaders through their own interactions with the person. Not surprisingly, within a couple of years, he was promoted twice.

A direct interaction with influential individuals helps to establish a person's presence.

In my career, I grabbed numerous opportunities to interact and dialogue with senior executives through engaging in projects, which were not part of my normal responsibilities. For example, I volunteered to spend four months working directly with a senior counsel to finalize a business partnership agreement. I worked two months directly with the president of my company to finalize a joint venture strategy. I often studied business plans issued by other departments and provided my viewpoints to them without being asked. I occasionally sent my ideas and questions to senior executives about improvement opportunities.

Not everyone is fortunate enough to have the opportunities I had to engage in special projects, and not everyone has the appropriate skills to get involved. "How can I get more involved in special projects?" you may ask.

Here is one of many answers. Once, a senior executive shared his success stories with a group of employees. He said although he was an engineer by trade he read business and financial magazines such as *The Wall Street Journal*, *Forbes*, and *The Economist* as a hobby. Over time, he developed a strong business sense. As a result, he added value when he was in conversations with his boss, peers, and other business leaders, and naturally he was given the opportunities to do things that mattered to other people and the company.

Active participation in team discussions is an essential duty of all employees. Truly, actively contributing to meeting discussions marks an employees' presence and in turn builds up their circle of influence over time. I personally have missed numerous opportunities to contribute to the success of my company by holding back my thoughts in group meetings. I was brought up in a culture where people were encouraged to say things only when they were certain, and people believed that a bucket half-full, or a person who failed to know all the facts, only "made loud, annoying noise."

In the corporate world, being too conservative and too quiet limits people's ability to achieve goals and contribute to the bigger community.

4.2   Be Alert of Potential Dangers

Early in my career, the influence circle I had was small and I only needed to focus on my own areas of work. As I became more senior in the company, my work became more dependent on my collaboration with other groups and interaction with people became increasingly important.

When I began working in China, my mentor, with whom I had the utmost trust, gave me some advice. He said, "All it takes is one person who dislikes you to ruin your career." I had mixed feelings when I heard his advice. First, I thought he exaggerated. Second, his comment certainly was true for not only in China but also everywhere around the world. After I heard his comment, I started changing my work habits. I gradually spent more time looking out for unexpected events and dangers that might put me in vulnerable situations.

Dangers or problems may come from many different angles. For example, my peers from another department may break their commitments; my subordinates may forget to follow through with their actions; my boss may have forgotten about his previous conversations with me leading to misunderstandings; and I may commit unintentional mistakes.

I remember vividly a situation in which a member of my staff unknowingly overlooked a small matter causing me to form a judgment about her – that she had low standards. She had asked me to consider hiring her nephew as a student apprentice during his summer break. Her nephew was in the last year of his undergraduate university program. If my company hired him, it would be a win-win situation for all. However, her nephew's resume had numerous spelling mistakes, was poorly formatted, and lacked organization. After I had told my staff member about the problems with the resume, she told me that her nephew decided to withdraw his internship application.

My staff member committed a couple of mistakes in this endeavor. First, the poor quality of her nephew's resume reflected on her own quality standards. My belief was that if my staff had high quality standards, she would have helped improve her nephew's resume before passing it to me. Second, my staff did not try her best to help her nephew. If she did, she would have coached her nephew on how to best present his case to get the job. In the end, her nephew gave up after one challenge I had raised about his resume. My staff member's original intention of helping her nephew inadvertently created a bad impression of herself.

Have you done enough to protect yourself from potential dangers?

My mentor told me another piece of great advice: "If people want to find your problems, they will first analyze your expense reimbursement reports. So, make sure that you make no mistake in your expense reports."

I followed my mentor's advice and I did more. For example, I made efforts to carefully show my colleagues that I did not misuse company benefits. When I treated colleagues from another department to lunch, I destroyed the restaurant receipt in front of them to show that the lunch was on my own personal expense.

I also made efforts to minimize spending of company money to create a positive personal image. For example, I occasionally travelled by economy class while my company allowed for business class international air travel.

In addition, I occasionally did not use company benefits that were insignificant. For my job assignment in China, my company allowed me to take my wife for a trip from Shanghai to Hong Kong for rest-and-relaxation once a year. The trip was qualified for business class air travel. However, I did not take the rest-and-relaxation benefit for a few years, and for the years I did take the trip, my wife and I travelled in economy class. I believed that I did not need the rest-and-relaxation trips every year and that for a three-hour trip, my wife and I could travel comfortably in economy class. My gesture to travel less frequently and more cost effectively created a positive and solid impression with my employer. The sacrifice I made in not using my full benefits was small, but the positive impact made on my boss was significant.

4.3   Be a Squeaky Wheel

"The squeaky wheel gets the grease," says a popular proverb. In the workplace, people who speak up loudly receive the attention, which they seek. I have seen many people who were too timid to ask for what they want and missed out on what they deserved.

Knowing when to "squeak" takes confidence and a strong sense of self-awareness.

If the "squeaking" is done appropriately and at the right frequency, employees will get what they deserve. For example, employees should ask for more responsibilities if they become more skilled at their work; they should ask for a mentor if they want one; they should ask for advice and opinions if they come across critical decisions; and they should ask to change their job assignments if they feel that they have become stagnant in their current jobs.

I have always encouraged my subordinates to sign up for company sponsored training and educational assistance programs, which are natural ways for them to "squeak" loudly. Once they have applied for the programs, they will receive attention from the management team. During the program approval process, their values and performances will be evaluated and discussed. They may or may not be selected for the programs. Nonetheless, they make themselves known to the management team by signing-up.

4.4 Avoid Being a High Maintenance Employee

In the workplace, the term "high maintenance" is often used to describe those employees who need constant attention by their leaders to address their concerns, wants, and needs. For example, a high maintenance employee may unreasonably ask for salary increases too often; they may have too many demands from the company; they may not uphold core company values in their day-to-day interactions with customers; they may consistently require their leader's help to perform their jobs; they may require frequent senior management mediation to resolve their personal conflicts with other employees; or they may "squeak" excessively, becoming a constant nuisance.

In general, employees who are high maintenance inhibit their own career growths.

4.5 Enjoy Making Changes

One of my bosses once told me that my company hired me for only one reason: I was hired to make changes. He was correct. I believe that every employee is hired to change the company to become more productive, efficient, and profitable. If you are not making changes, your value to your company will be insignificant.

Think about the job you are doing today. Are you leading any changes?

- If you are a senior executive, you could be continuously thinking about evolving your organization's vision and strategies to address the ever changing economy and customer demands.
- If you are a director, you could be leading your organization to improve productivity or to increase the customer base.

- If you are a supervisor, you could be leading your teams to improve manufacturing efficiency or providing better service.
- If you are an individual team member, you could be contributing to better the customer experience or improve the work environment.

Everything you do is about making changes.

Change is an essential and necessary constant in any company. Therefore, If you are not leading or participating in any change evolving around the company, or worse yet, if you are resistant to change, you provide little value to the company and your job is destined to become extinct.

4.6 Safeguard Your Reputation

A good reputation is hard to earn, yet easy to be destroyed.

It is important to safeguard your reputation, especially during job transitions. Many people have a wrong focus during job transitions – they prioritize and invest their time in preparing for the new job, paying less effort on the existing one.

When transitioning from one job to another, I always prioritize wrapping up perfectly my old job instead of preparing for the new job. I make sure that I do not give my successors any opportunity to talk poorly about me, as it is very easy for them to complain what does not work and what can be improved. Successors will find problems with their predecessors' work and make changes.

Let's look at this situation from another perspective.

When you get a new job, you normally have a honeymoon period during which time you gain knowledge about the new environment, you learn what has been done before, you identify the changes you need to make, and you probably need to fix the problems that your predecessor left behind. And naturally, it is a perfect opportunity for you to tell others how bad a job your predecessor has done – anything that is not perfect, you can blame on your predecessor.

Hence, in order to maintain your best professional image and uphold your good will, when you leave your existing job, you need to make sure that you leave a good legacy behind.

When I worked in a technology company many years ago, I changed my job assignments at least once every two years. Changing job assignments frequently was one way to keep my skills current and to prevent me from becoming stagnant on any job. In every job transition, I spent a lot of time documenting my work, transferring my knowledge to my peers, laying out the steps for the unfinished career plans of my subordinates, and organizing relevant emails, reports, and address-book contacts for my successors' future reference.

I remember that, for one project, I unofficially helped my successor for six months after I had left the job. My efforts in ensuring that my successors were successful not only protected my previous employees and my hard-earned reputation, but also strengthened many personal connections, which helped my career growth tremendously.

One of my subordinates impressed me even before I hired him. In China, employees need to notify their employers at least one month in advance for their job resignations. Normally, one month is a long time to wait for the hiring company. In this case, when I extended my job offer to the candidate, he asked me to allow him two months to finish off and properly transition a critical project before he would join my company. His request initially seemed unreasonable. However, he demonstrated his loyalty to his existing employer and his passion for his work. I loved his style and attitude and consequently I loved to have him work for me.

4.7 Develop Self-awareness

Can you guess accurately how you rank in your organization from your boss' point of view?

Do you know if you have a good boss or are working at a good company?

Do you know if you have a good career ahead of you or are wasting time in a role where you are not going anywhere regardless of what you do?

If you have a higher degree of self-awareness, you would probably have clearer answers of the above. A lack of self-awareness limits your career growth.

I would leave it to you to find effective ways to improve your self-awareness. In general, you can gradually improve your self-awareness if you are humble, have a high curiosity, and are sensitive to changes and loopholes around the company.

4.8   Benefit from a Mentor

I once read a report which suggested that many leaders become successful because they have mentors. I agree wholeheartedly.

In mentorship, there are many different relationship levels. In general, mentors and mentees engage in frequent dialogue. Through active exchanges of information and opinions, mentors provide guidance and advice to mentees on problem solving, career planning, and professional development.

I have seen many successful mentoring relationships in the corporate workplace, where mentors actively help their mentees to become very successful in their careers. Since mentors typically hold a more senior job position within a company, there are a few things mentors can easily do within their circles of influence to give their mentees an advantage over other employees.

For example, mentors could:

- Help to make their mentees more visible to the management circle by adding a voice of support or recommendation.
- Eliminate roadblocks for their mentees to successfully deliver their work.
- Based on their higher level of authority, bring their mentees to strategic meetings and assign them to take on certain jobs which are otherwise not accessible to the mentees.
- Provide influential references to support their mentees' job applications.

One success story worth mentioning is that I once knew a young professional whose mentor was a senior vice president. He was promoted by the company, under strong influences of his mentor, three times within two years, from a senior engineer to a director. He was subsequently sponsored by the company to participate in an Executive MBA program at a world-renowned university in the United States.

Unfortunately, not every mentoring relationship works.

A mentoring relationship is a personal engagement between two people sustained over a long period of time. This means that if there is a personality conflict, the relationship will not last. If either one party does not treat the relationship as a priority, it will not last.

I treasure all the mentoring relationships I had with my mentors. Although no relationship lasts forever, I have been able to sustain all mentoring relationships for long periods of time by holding on to two basic principles:

1. I maximize the personality match with my mentors by identifying the people whom I respect and humbly invite them to be my mentors.
2. I maximize the interactions with my mentors by proactively setting up face-to-face meetings with them on a frequent basis.

Finding a mentor is not hard. All you need to do is to find a person whom you admire and are comfortable working with, and simply ask. You would be surprised by the large number of senior leaders who are willing to help junior employees.

In China, there is a more intimate level of mentoring relationship – a relationship that goes beyond the normal business engagement of mentors and mentees. In such a relationship, mentors are referred to as Masters and mentees are referred to as Apprentices.

Masters commit to teach their apprentices everything they know and apprentices commit to learn everything that their masters teach them. Masters are life coaches and the relationship can last for a lifetime. There is one unspoken practice between masters and apprentices. That is, apprentices may not have the freedom to choose which advice to listen to and which advice to ignore. Often, if apprentices do not like a suggestion from their masters or are uncomfortable with doing what their masters have told them, the apprentices are obliged to follow the directives regardless. Not trying would jeopardize the relationship. There is an ultimate level of commitment and respect in the relationship.

Finding a master who is willing to teach me everything about his wisdom has been one of my dreams. So far, I have not been successful. In fact, many years ago, I nearly found a master but I failed to convince him to accept me as his apprentice. I mistakenly did not follow through with a couple advices which I felt uncomfortable following. It was a mistake on my part because I failed to realize that I was not equipped with sufficient information to appreciate his advice at the time.

In working with mentors, we have to understand that mentors may not be able to tell us all the reasons behind their advice due to confidentiality, that the advice may only be appropriate to be given out informally, that it may be unethical to pass down certain information, or that the mentor may judge that it is more appropriate to not let the mentees to know the reasons. As mentees, we may have to honor our total trust and act out on the advice.

The benefits of a successful mentoring relationship are obvious. Hence, my advice to my readers is that they find a mentor if they do not have one yet.

4.9 Communicate to Reinforce Your Professional Image

I see every piece of communication as an opportunity for me to reinforce my professional image!

It takes a long time to build a positive professional image. However, it only takes one incidence of poor communication to destroy a good image.

I am especially cautious in communicating using email. Email is a convenient and effective communication tool when used properly. However, there are many inherent problems associated with the use of email because it is a one-way conversation, and I cannot see the reaction of the person reading the email. To build and reinforce my professional image, I have a few self-inflicted guidelines when writing emails.

1. I do not translate facts into negative personal judgments because one-way accusations and judgments always give rise to disputes and conflicts, which corrode trust and teamwork. For example, when a person ignores a step in a business process, I simply state that fact instead of accusing the person for violating a company policy. When a person denies a commitment, I simply state that fact instead of blaming the person for low integrity. When a person consistently takes long lunch breaks and leaves work

early, I simply state that fact instead of labeling the person as lazy.

2. For important messages that need not be sent immediately, I write the emails and leave them overnight. I don't send them until the next day. My mind is most active in the morning. When I wake up in the morning, all sorts of ideas rush to mind. So far, almost without exception, I have been able to refine the emails I have written the day before and improve on them before I send them out.

3. If being the first to send an email is important, I treat it as the top priority and even sacrifice my own personal time to get it done. Occasionally, it is important for me to take control to convey a piece of good news, to describe a problem, or to report a crisis. Being the first to communicate allows me to paint the situation accurately for others to interpret so as to preempt others from presenting the situation inaccurately. By being first to communicate, I hold a more proactive and controlling position.

4. I ensure that the list of people on the email distribution is appropriate. A common mistake I frequently made, no matter how careful I had been, was that I replied an email to everyone on the distribution unintentionally while my response was intended for just the sender. By observing my subordinates' email communication, I found that the more junior the employees, the more mistakes they

made in email distribution lists. They often sent their email to more people than necessary.

5. I assume that all my emails will not be kept confidential. In the corporate world, there is no such thing as a private email. I have learned from my experience that my emails can be forwarded to everyone in the company by the recipients intentionally or unintentionally, no matter how I restrict the distribution by marking it "private", "do not forward", or "confidential".

6. I always keep my email short and to the point. This ensures that my recipients have a higher chance of reading my entire email even if they are occupied with other priorities. In fact, writing short, concise emails requires more thoughts and takes more efforts than writing long ones as emphasized by Mark Twain, "I didn't have time to write a short letter, so I wrote a long one instead."

I have spent a lot of effort ensuring my subordinates present a professional image. As a result, I protect my own professional image. Theoretically, I own all the work that is delivered by my team. If my subordinates deliver low quality work, they reflect on the whole team's quality image. Therefore, one of my priorities has been to coach my subordinates on making sure that their emails and presentation materials carry consistent and accurate information with no spelling mistakes.

Any email I forward from my subordinates becomes my work, even though I did not write the emails initially. That is, if the forwarded email contains information that is non-factual, I am also responsible for spreading the rumor; if the forwarded email presents a decision, I also agree with the decision on the forwarded email unless I specifically say otherwise.

Hence, when I need to forward any message from my subordinates to others, it is essential and necessary for me to make sure that their work is accurate and up to professional standards. I either correct all the mistakes in their emails or presentation materials before I forward them, or I write an executive summary to properly introduce their work.

4.10 Strike a Balance

Explaining your actions versus not

Have you ever come across situations where you were wrongly judged by others and have a burning desire to explain your actions?

In my career, I have had many unavoidable personal conflicts with my colleagues and there have been rumors or accusations about me that were not supported by factual events. I found that, often, the best way to deal with conflicts and inappropriate accusations is not to defend the situations.

I have found that when I make mistakes, the best action to take is to apologize in a confident manner and move on.

There were many times when I tried to explain the reasons behind my actions, I inadvertently fell into the trap of attempting to find excuses to defend my actions and justify my mistakes. The more I explained, the more I tried to find excuses that were unreasonable and unacceptable to others and the less professional I became. That's why I always believe that when I start explaining, I have already lost.

I remember many years ago when I worked as an engineer, I was concerned about how my boss and my peers viewed my job performance. I tried to make sure that my actions were well understood and accepted by others. One day, my boss questioned why I picked one solution to address a problem instead of another, and I gave him a quick answer. He nodded and left my office. After he left, I felt an urge to explain more. I subsequently spent four hours writing a two-page email to my boss. To my surprise, he replied to me with a short sentence saying that he did not expect to receive a long essay from me since I had already given him the answer when we had spoken earlier. I wasted four hours and achieved nothing positive.

Making a good judgment on when one needs to explain a situation takes experience. The more confidence I have, the more instances I found it unnecessary for me to explain my actions.

Replying responsively versus not

I have found that people who are consistently unresponsive to emails typically lack enthusiasm in doing their job and lack customer focus. They leave the sender of the email hanging with uncertainties:

- Was the lack of response an indication of agreement, disagreement, or no comment?
- Was the matter on hand not important?
- Had the recipient forgotten to respond?
- Were the recipients too busy to respond or did they not respond because they did not pay the due respect to the sender?

If there is an urgency to respond to an email, reply immediately. Often, a delayed response is viewed by the recipient as a no response as the information carried by the email could become immaterial because a decision or judgment has already been established due to the delay of the response.

Not every email needs to be replied to. Nonetheless, I have found that a timely, short response like "Thank you," "I agree," "Got it," "Received," "Well done," "Your request is noted and I will reply back to you tomorrow," "I have read it and I have no comments," or "(a smiley face symbol)," minimizes confusions and enhances the clarity of communications.

Being responsive is an essential professional attitude. In fact, being unresponsive is unacceptable.

Investing time to understand versus being quick to judge

The more senior a position we hold, the more judgments we make. One of the many attributes of a successful leader is the ability to make high quality judgments.

For a long time, I have tried to coach my subordinates on making judgments. I have had various degrees of success. The essence is that making good judgments requires a solid foundation of work experience and personal maturity. To correct my subordinates' judgments requires that I am patient, and I invest time to listen to their thoughts and share my experiences.

Judgment is subjective.

One of my subordinates was a sentimental person. He often made business decisions based on his likes and dislikes. For example, his decisions were often skewed to the wrong side when he pre-occupied his thoughts with the personality and behaviors of the person with whom he was dealing – thoughts regarding that the person was incapable or had a different personal agenda. My advice to him was that he needed to slow down so that he could make objective business decisions instead of quick subjective, often emotional, judgments.

It is important and necessary for leaders to draw a balance when making judgments. In general, it is important that we invest time, which we may not have, to understand the differences and more importantly, the similarities of opinions, instead of being quick to doubt and disapprove of other people's actions and opinions.

Adapting to Workplace Dynamics

Summary of key points:

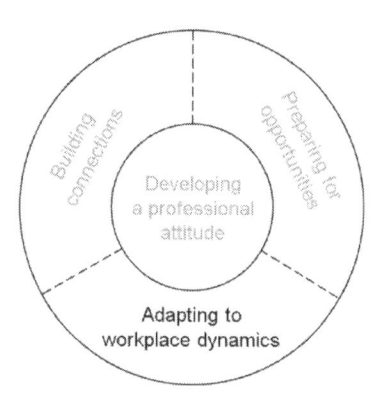

1. In order to increase your chances to be around at the right place at the right time, you need to make an effort to be around all the time. (Page 72)

2. Participate in meetings actively. In the corporate workplace, being too conservative and too quiet limits your ability to achieve goals and contribute to the bigger community. (Page 75)

3. Look out for unexpected events and dangers that might put you in vulnerable situations. (Page 76)

4. Ask for what you want and deserve while avoid being a high maintenance employee. (Page 78)

5. Actively seek work that changes the company to become more productive, efficient, and profitable. (Page 80)

6. When you leave your existing job, wrap up your job well to maintain your best professional image and uphold your good will. (Page 82)

7. Find a mentor and actively nourish the relationship to secure an advantage over your peers. (Page 84)

8. When you make mistakes, the best action to take is to apologize in a confident manner and move on. (Page 91)

9. Being responsive is an essential professional attitude. Reply your emails promptly to show your enthusiasm and customer focus, and most importantly your decisiveness and clear thinking. (Page 93)

10. Invest time to understand the differences and more importantly, the similarities of opinions, instead of being quick to doubt and disapprove of other people's actions and opinions. (Page 94)

Loyalty is the top consideration in selecting people to work for me.

5

Connecting with Your Boss

5.1   Be Loyal to Your Boss

When it comes to connecting to your boss, the first thing that comes to mind is loyalty.

In an earlier chapter, I have said that it is good for young professionals to seek work with a number of companies, but only change companies with a frequency that sustains an image of being loyal. I will leave it to you to determine the right amount of change appropriate to your own situations. However, once you decide to stay in your job, you should have an all-in attitude to work with your boss.

In my career, I have been fortunate in that nearly all of my previous bosses were competent professionals. Only three of them lacked capability and had low integrity.

If I cannot be loyal, I leave my boss.

There are two types of bosses I do not enjoy working with: those who have low integrity and those who are incompetent. If my boss has low integrity, I quit my job immediately. I either change jobs within the same company or seek job opportunities elsewhere. When I have incompetent bosses I make a decision on whether the best option is to leave or to continue working for them. If it is worthwhile to follow them, I will be loyal and will help them as much as I can.

Being loyal and having an all-in attitude to help my bosses is one reason for my success. Being loyal means protecting my bosses' interests, helping them recover from their mistakes, and assisting them to achieve business goals. This attitude guides my priorities and the way I deliver my work. It naturally fuels my internal drive to do the best in my job.

Once, one of my bosses told me his definition of the best boss-subordinate relationship. He said, "The best relationship is one when the subordinate knows exactly what the boss has in mind and does whatever it takes to address what's in the boss' mind without being asked by the boss."

Such a trusting relationship is extremely difficult to achieve as it requires the subordinate to know the boss' personality and style and it can only be achieved after a long time working together. In fact, my boss was hinting that he and I had reached that level of relationship. In my career, I had come across two bosses who had given me the ultimate trust to do whatever I believed was right without consulting them for advance approvals.

I would like to provide another example to reinforce the importance of being loyal. A senior executive of a multinational company advised me that an employee who gets their boss into trouble should be fired. What a pragmatic advice! Loyal employees would not intentionally get their boss into trouble.

A CEO of a major software company once shared with me an analogy. He told me that hypothetically, employees could be divided into three groups.

1. Employees who act based on their own interpretations of company goals and what's good for the company.
2. Employees who act based on their bosses' directives.
3. Employees who act based on their own personal agendas.

He would, without hesitation, prefer working with the group who follows their bosses' directives.

Being loyal has opened up numerous opportunities for me and has been a powerful way for me to connect with my bosses.

I remember many years ago both my boss and I attended the same leadership training class designed for senior leaders of our company. There were about twenty participants, all had prior interactions with each other and knew each other quite well. The instructor poured onto a table a few hundred index-cards. Written on each index-card was a word describing one attribute of leadership style, such as, commitment, quality, focus, passion, courage, discernment, dominance, and humility. Every participant was asked to pick out index-cards to give to other participants describing the latter's leadership attributes. I watched as my boss searched through the pile of cards. To my surprise, my boss took an index-card, crossed out the word written on it, wrote down the word "loyal", and passed it secretly to me.

5.2 Frame the Perception

The first impression is the deepest!

When you have established a judgment or perception on another person, you will continue to bear the same judgment during future interactions with the person. It takes a long time and much effort for the judgment to be changed. Judgment is like a filter lens used in photography. The effect can be an exaggeration of certain colors or a distortion of certain images.

Once a judgment or filter lens has been established, a boss will subconsciously put on the same filter lens to interact with his subordinate. Examples of these filter lenses could be:

- Smart
- Hardworking
- Resourceful
- Strategic
- Knowledgeable

- Lazy
- Immature

Whenever I work for a new boss, I always focus on crafting the right lens for my new boss to judge me. Crafting a lens is not difficult. All it needs is some deliberate effort.

On a new job assignment or project, I always put in a little bit of overtime so that I can be seen by my colleagues and my boss as a hardworking person. I try hard to be active in all activities, including meetings, discussions, and company organized social activities, and show a high degree of curiosity of the business and a strong connection with other employees.

In fact, as I spend extra effort to consciously craft the lenses, I build good habits. For example, I have a habit of being punctual, delivering high-quality work, and avoiding spelling mistakes. As time went by, these habits shaped my professional image and who I am.

Throughout my career, I have tried hard to make sure that the best of my behaviors are visible to my bosses and colleagues so that they can talk about me and judge me favorably.

For example, I enjoy going to work early so that I can plan through my day's work before the busy day begins. For a period of time I made sure that I was the first one to arrive at the office. This meant that I had to be in the office around 6:00am. This habit has worked wonders for me for a couple of reasons.

First, bosses typically come to work early. The early morning greetings of "Hello" or "Good Morning" marked my presence and led to occasional casual conversations with my bosses.

Second, as I was always the first person arriving at the office, I effectively created something for everyone in the office including my peers, my subordinates, and the housekeeping personnel to talk about. These small conversations about me helped my professional image. Actually, it is easy to understand that being the second person arriving in the office does not work, as it is not interesting to talk about a person who is the second one arriving in the office.

When I was young, I made every effort to convince my company to sponsor me to attend training classes. I have found that many employers do not mind spending extra investment to sponsor their employees on training. Attending training classes not only enriched my skills and knowledge but also promoted my visibility to the management team.

Many companies sponsor their employees for MBA degrees. Due to the high cost of MBA classes, typically only one or a handful of employees are selected to participate in the sponsorship. I have learned that almost without exception, it is worthwhile to apply for the MBA or higher degree sponsorships whether one is qualified or not. The reason is that even if the application is unsuccessful, the applicants would have successfully framed a positive perception for the management team to judge them favorably.

One subordinate of mine effectively did something unusual. He signed up for a doctorate degree when he was forty-five years old. Another subordinate who worked in Korea with twenty years of work experience under his belt told me that he started to learn Putonghua, the Chinese official language. Both of them successfully impressed their peers and me of their passion in learning and personal development.

Finding the right situation to show your boss that you try to reduce the company's costs and spending is always worthwhile.

I remember an international business trip where I had to travel with my boss from the US to China. For such long international air trips, employees were allowed to travel on business class. However, considering that the company business was not performing well, an economy class air ticket would save the company 75% of my trip's costs, and as I was traveling with my boss, it was the perfect time for me to craft a lens for my boss to correctly judge me.

I booked an economy class ticket for myself without informing my boss ahead of time. The little discomfort traveling in economy class paid off. For the rest of my career working for this boss, he trusted my work and judgment on controlling costs.

5.3   Promote Your Visibility

In the business world, it is important that your boss has something unique to talk about you. Being visible, especially to the senior management team is an essential step to getting recognized and rewarded.

I have seen numerous junior departmental managers fail to convince the senior management leadership team to approve their subordinates for job promotions. A typical problem is that the person being recommended for promotion is not known to the rest of the management leadership team. As a result, there is a lack of support for the recommendation.

Realizing the need to be visible beyond my own department, I always tried to find opportunities to do something extraordinary so that my boss has something interesting to talk about me. Sometimes, doing extraordinary things would require a little bit of innovative thinking and some risk-taking.

Once, I was asked to lead a team of engineers to develop a telecommunication product which would provide voice and video services to people's homes. My first task was to lead a team of engineers to develop a ten-page proposal on the feasibility of the product within one week. Realizing that this was a rare opportunity for me to do something extraordinary, I held a workshop with my team and developed the ten-page proposal. In addition, I led the team to produce a 140-page report on the functional design of the product, based on a lot of assumptions.

Under a normal project schedule, the functional design was not due until three months later when all the assumptions would have been verified and validated. If the team made the wrong assumptions, the functional design would be wrong and the design effort would be wasted. I took the risk of being accused of not following the routine process and submitted the 140-page functional design document to my boss.

Indeed, my boss was amazed that the team was capable of producing the functional design within one week, as opposed to three months into the schedule. He was so impressed that he sent my functional design to the director and the vice president of my organization.

Everyone too was impressed!

People were simply fascinated by the details within the report and the lightning speed of my work. No one cared if I followed the normal process guidelines. No one questioned the accuracy of the assumptions which formed the foundation of the functional design. To me, it really did not matter if I needed to redo the functional design. The outcome was great. The one-week investment was worthwhile to me and to the company as I fast tracked the product development cycle, whilst successfully creating a story for the senior management team to say "Wow" about me. I made myself visible.

On another occasion, I did something extraordinary based on my own assessment of needs.

I was an engineer working in a team responsible for assessing the feasibility of expanding our research and development capabilities from Canada to China. The intention was that within two years we would hire 500 local Chinese nationals, trained to be capable of conducting advance product research in China. In one group meeting, the team discussed how to recruit people and how to train new employees. During the meeting, I volunteered to draft a training plan for the new recuits and review this plan with the team within one week.

To impress the team, I realized that I needed to do more than I had promised. Hence, in addition to developing a training plan, I decided to also design a training curriculum, which was of equal importance as the training plan. I worked fourteen hours a day that week and compiled a detailed training curriculum comprising more than fifty training classes, each with a full description of the class objective and contents. My boss and my peers were pleasantly surprised, since no one had the knowledge to completely define the curriculum and its contents. However, to everyone's surprise I did it quickly.

One week after I delivered the training plan and the curriculum to my boss, he and I had a discussion over dinner. He told me that his boss was extremely pleased with my work. His boss had asked him: "Where does this guy come from? He is amazing!" From then on, the senior management team knew me well!

Doing something unusual is not difficult.

For example, a colleague of mine once did a 360-degree feedback, which created a ripple of discussions within the senior management team. A 360-degree feedback requires that employees ask their bosses, peers, and subordinates to provide them written candid feedback. Based on the feedback, actions are developed to improve their leadership skills. It is a good tool to increase self-awareness and for personal development. Before my colleague conducted his 360-degree feedback, no one else in the company had done it. Being the first employee to humbly take part in a 360-degree feedback, my colleague successfully impressed his boss with his creativity and learning attitude.

There is no lack of innovative ways to make one visible in a workplace.

For example, during my long career, there were a few periods of time I dressed more neatly and professionally than my peers to work. In particular, I have worked for three major companies and none of them required their employees to wear ties to work. I seized the opportunity to be different from the rest of the crowd. In one instance, I was one of a few people who wore a tie to work. I did that for a period of two years, long enough to secure a consistent positive image on everyone in the company. It is hard for me to estimate the impact of this small act. However, I am sure that by simply wearing a tie, I most likely created a more professional and mature image than that of not wearing one; an image my bosses occasionally loved to talk about.

5.4 Do Not Shoot Yourself in the Foot

Trust and credibility can only be earned with time and effort, yet they can be destroyed by just one careless or thoughtless act.

A couple of habits of mine have helped my professional image and career tremendously.

First, whenever I have discussions and reach alignment with my boss, I make sure that I follow through with doing what my boss and I had agreed. Following through and completing all my committed actions is important as it ensures that my boss feels good about his time spent with me. On the other hand, if my boss feels that his time with me has been wasted because I did not follow through, he will feel that I failed to learn and he will lose his interest in coaching me again.

For example, for something as small as changing information on a slide of a presentation, I make sure that I do not forget about any changes that my boss and I had previously discussed.

Several times, my subordinates left me bad impressions by implementing actions that contradict what we had previously agreed. In one instance, I instructed my subordinate to send out meeting minutes after every project review. However, she failed to send meeting minutes for all meetings. For those meeting minutes she missed, she argued that there was nothing interesting to report. In my mind, not sending some of the meeting minutes meant that she ignored her earlier agreement with me, she created inconsistency in her communications with the project team, and she failed.

In another instance, my subordinate agreed that he needed to call a sales manager to rectify a situation. Yet, after our agreement, he changed his mind without checking back with me again. Instead of phoning the sales manager, he wrote an email. It was an insignificant change he had thought. However, by not using the telephone, he negated his prior agreement with me, and he missed the chance to have an interactive dialogue with the sales manager.

I always know when I need to consult with my boss and when I can freely do my own thing. My principle has been that once I start asking my boss for advice on how to resolve an issue, I have to respect his advice until the issue is resolved. For matters that I do not ask for advice, I can continue to be innovative and freely do them my way.

Hence, once I ask my bosses for help, I always do exactly what we have agreed. If better ideas come to mind later, I will not implement the better ideas without consulting my bosses again. In fact, the more I consult with my bosses, the more help I receive from them and the more trust I build. By consulting my bosses frequently, I learn their value systems and their understanding of the company big pictures, which help me to be more confident in acting on my own.

A seemingly harmless small act can damage trust with the boss.

I remember I once asked my subordinate to make a sales pitch at a project meeting because he had the best presentation skills and he knew the presentation materials best. I needed him to do it for two reasons. First, I needed him to have active interactions with other senior members of the project team so that I could have more support when I wanted to promote him later. Second, I needed my strongest staff to make the sales pitch so as to strengthen the professional image of my department. However, he failed to see these two important points.

After he had agreed to make the sales pitch, he shot himself in the foot by delegating the presentation to his staff without consulting me again. My subordinate's reason was that he would like to train his staff and give them the opportunity. However, he failed to realize that by not following through with our agreed actions, he had violated the trust between us, which would be difficult to fully regain.

Second, once I have convinced my boss to accept my idea, I have an obligation and an opportunity to demonstrate my skills. No matter how small the task, it becomes my top priority to deliver the best results and cover all contingencies to follow through in executing my idea.

Here is an interesting example. One of my bosses I used to work for had a strong mind and he liked to be in full-control of all situations. One summer, I planned to have a vacation with my family for one week during a very demanding time at work. In particular, the project I was leading had an important milestone to be delivered. Although I was extremely confident that I could take the vacation and deliver the project at the same time, I had a tough decision to make. I had to decide whether I should cancel my vacation with my family, which was planned and scheduled four months in advance or convince my boss that allowing me to take the vacation was a right decision on his part.

After my boss and I had had a short discussion about my vacation, he allowed me to go. But, I knew exactly what would happen after I came back from my vacation. Knowing his style, he would ask me detailed questions about the project upon my return, in an attempt to prove to me that I should not have taken the vacation. I also realized that this could be a rare opportunity for me to impress him. However, the risk was high. That is, if I failed to impress him, or if he did not ask me questions upon my return from my vacation, I could have left him with a non-erasable negative impression forever.

I went on my vacation with my family as planned. Every day during my vacation, I sacrificed a couple of hours to check all my emails and stay in tune with the pulse of the project. The evening when I returned home from my vacation, I called the project team for a four-hour face-to-face meeting to review every detail of the project. I was prepared for my boss' summoning the next day. As anticipated, the next morning when I returned to my office, my boss asked me to meet with him. He spent half an hour asking me questions about the project, from important to trivial matters. And, I impressed him with all the details he requested. After this encounter, the trusting relationship between us got even stronger.

5.5 Connect with Bad Bosses

During a life-long career, it is unavoidable that we face bad bosses who take advantage of their subordinates, have low integrity, are unreasonable in their demands, are incompetent, or are simply immature. It is important that we know how to work with them.

When I interact with bad bosses, I always tell myself that I have only two choices:

1. Leave them.
2. Stay with them and find a way to enjoy the working relationship.

There is no third option.

That is, staying with a bad boss and suffering and complaining about them would not work. In fact, I have a unique opinion about bad bosses. I view the working relationship with them as an opportunity for me to improve my skills – skills that I cannot learn from a good boss.

Based on my observation, the majority of bosses are great people who have earned their leadership positions. Thus, whenever I tumble into a bad boss, I view it as a fortunate situation and I make the best use of the opportunity to enjoy the rare moments of dealing with them.

I remember that during the first ten years of my career, I was young and professionally immature. I had one boss who, from what I could judge, was lazy and did not pay attention to details. He took his subordinates' achievements and claimed them to be his own. He spent most of his time building relationships with his bosses and peers, instead of doing real work. In my mind, other than being able to articulate his viewpoints and secure strong relationships with his co-workers, he was incompetent.

Concerned that my boss could hinder my career, I discussed my worry with my mentor who was a director of my company. To my surprise, my mentor passed along to me a great wisdom. He said, "You think your boss is bad because you are still too young and inexperienced to see beyond what you already know. But, have you ever thought about what skills have led him to his success today? Your boss will be very successful in his career."

After my conversation with my mentor, it struck me that I could have misjudged my boss. I thought he was bad. However, my mentor counter argued that my boss had skills that I could learn. Indeed, when I was young, I felt that some of the job promotions could have been given to me instead of to others who were older and had higher seniority within the company. And, I blindly labeled them as incompetent bad bosses.

It was fortunate that I learned my mentor's wisdom early enough in my career. Taking my mentor's advice, I changed my attitude in interacting with bad bosses. I always try to learn how bad bosses manage to "survive" and excel in their careers. Without exception, I learned from every one of the bad bosses. I learned skills on how to better communicate, delegate, build relationships, and simply work smarter. More importantly, I learned how to connect with them based on who they were.

The toughest situation I experienced was when my boss plainly did not like me, and I had to offensively deal with the situation. I remember one boss who had only one objective in his mind: he wanted to fire me. Before he was promoted to be the leader of my team, he was my peer and we did not get along. We both worked in an IT organization responsible for developing tools to improve employee productivity. He had a Bachelor degree in financial management with only limited knowledge of information technology. Hence, when he and I were peers, his performance was inferior to mine. His advantage was his wealth of experience: he had twenty years of experience and I had ten.

After he was promoted and became my boss, he was on a mission to fire me. He started to ask me to deliver work with milestones that were impossible to meet. He questioned every key action I took. He persistently disapproved my ideas that I believed were necessary and innovative. Facing his unpleasant attitude, I tried for three months to build a relationship with him, but I was unsuccessful. My only way out was to take on an offensive mode and deal with his attitude and behavior directly. I by-passed him and went to his manager, a director, with one goal in mind. Either I would successfully make a case for myself or I would quit the company. I had only one chance to strike. For this case, my strike was accurate and forceful. The director asked me to stay, and he fired my boss two months after our discussion.

Knowing how to judge whether a boss is a good or a bad one, and what to learn and not to learn from a boss is critical to your career success.

I remember I once inherited a group of employees. One person had a few inappropriate habits, of which he was unaware. For example, he did not spend company money wisely. In particular, he consumed many expensive alcoholic drinks inappropriately on business trips. His email communication was not precise and of poor quality, and he did not act with a sense of urgency when required. I pointed out to him that he had picked up these inappropriate habits from his previous leader, whom he respected as his role model. It took him a long time to correct these inappropriate behaviors, which would otherwise prevent his career growth.

Good bosses should be good coaches and should take care of their subordinates' professional skill development. Thus, if you are still young and ambitious and you are not learning from your boss and not growing your experience, it is time to leave your boss and the company. I have seen many people who stay with their boss learning nothing and wasting precious time in the early yet critical times of their career journey.

5.6 Package Your Message

A long time ago, I learned a tactic from a business magazine about how to package bad news and good news for delivery. This tactic has helped me to connect with my bosses tremendously.

You should bundle all the bad news together and tell the boss all of them at once. That is, if your boss is going to be upset, let him or her be upset once and for all.

On the other hand, if you have a few pieces of good news to tell, you should convey them one at a time in separate sequential occasions. The reason is that continuously and persistently delivering good news to your boss in intermittent pulses reinforces the good message and the image of strong performance.

5.7 Communicate with a Purpose

It is strange that no matter how much and how frequent I communicate with my bosses, I almost always feel that I have not communicated enough. I believe that my personality has dictated my way of interacting with other people. I do not enjoy going to my bosses for casual conversations, so during the limited number of interactions with my bosses, I pay special attention to create a positive impression.

Let me begin with one example where a lack of communication led to a rough relationship between my boss and me, and how I recovered from the relationship.

My boss, who grew up leading factory workers, had a unique leadership style that I was not accustomed to. He was a director of the company. He enjoyed exercising his power and control. He had a dominant style and was impatient. For the first six months working with him, I was not able to communicate with him effectively. In fact, due to the difficulties in communication, we had had a misunderstanding about my job responsibilities and priorities. In addition, he got the wrong impression that I had not treated my subordinates with enough personal attention. With this negative perception of me from my boss, I desperately needed to find a way to break through the situation.

To create a breakthrough in my relationship with my boss, I started with the basics. My first step was to convince him that I was a good leader in the company. I made sure that I delivered business results; I informed him every step of my activities; and I developed a plan on how to evolve and develop my team. I focused on building his confidence in my capability and competence. Patiently, I waited for the breakthrough moment to come.

One day, during a one-on-one project discussion with my boss, I felt that he had lost his concentration. Something was troubling him. I thought my breakthrough moment might have just arrived. I stopped discussing the project and asked if something else was bothering him. He told me that he was worried about his mother who had been sick. He had to leave work early that day to take her to the hospital for a check-up. After I went home, I googled his mother's illness and incidentally came across a poem that I could use to comfort him.

That night, I sent the poem to my boss and expressed some of my inner thoughts. We exchanged a few emails. It was magic. From then on, my boss changed his perception and judgment of me. In relationship building, often, it takes persistence in carrying out a conversation, a dose of sincerity, and a caring heart.

One secretary I knew was extremely caring. Her boss had a habit of losing his pens. To help her boss, she kept about one hundred pens in a drawer. Whenever her boss asked for a pen, she opened up her drawer and invited her boss to pick a couple. I am sure it was unnecessary and was an exaggeration for the secretary to keep one hundred pens for her boss. However, the pens served as a special way for her to demonstrate how she cared for her boss.

We all communicate with a purpose. In the business world, we are not obliged to tell our colleagues everything about our personal lives. By telling our boss selective aspects of our lives, we can paint a positive image for them to judge us. Below is one example.

In order to increase personal interaction between project team members, a group of about thirty company employees were asked to share their personal profiles with one another. A personal profile is a presentation slide showing details about an employee's work experience, educational background, hobbies, family, and beliefs. The sharing was a lot of fun and it took about five minutes for each person.

Before the actual sharing, I reviewed a profile from one of my subordinates. He had written that one of his hobbies was drinking alcohol. I asked him to rethink what message and professional image he wanted to impress on his colleagues. I asked him to draft two profiles, one with and another without the reference of alcoholic drinks. With two printed profiles in front of him, he immediately realized that telling people that he enjoyed alcoholic drinks made his professional profile less impressive.

This is only one example of opportunities that allow us to tell our own true stories to our advantage.

Using the same example of sharing personal profiles, I could use the profile page to purposefully tell my peers and my boss the specific details that could influence their judgment on me. For example, I could talk about my family to emphasize that I value work-life balance; I could talk about my passion for solving brain-teaser puzzles to show my inclination in logical thinking and analysis; or I could talk about the period when I worked sixteen hours a day to show my dedication to the company.

One of the purposes of communication is to leave a positive professional impression.

One of my staff members loved shopping. The whole department knew this about her. One day, I asked her if she would want her subordinates to know and gossip about her shopping habits when she would be promoted to become a manager. Her answer was a fast and firm "No". Upon answering my question, she immediately realized that she did not want to be known for her shopping habits.

I always think about how to communicate with a positive tone. Often, there exists more than one way to describe a situation. For example, to describe a cup with water, certainly, saying "a cup half full" presents a more positive tone than saying "a cup half empty". Along the same vein, when there is crisis at work, I always look for opportunities to communicate with a tone of "a cup half full" rather than "a cup half empty".

Once, I successfully converted a crisis into an opportunity by forcefully and persistently communicating with my boss using a positive attitude.

In June 1999, I was the Chief Information Officer (CIO) of the China region of a multinational company. One of my responsibilities was to ensure that our corporate information was accurate and protected from cyber theft. In 1999, as the computing and telecommunication services and the professional knowledge of employees were still maturing in China, protecting corporate data was a challenge.

One day, while I was taking a vacation with my family outside the country, I received a telephone call from a member of my staff. He informed me that he had destroyed all the financial data along with the back-up data by committing a couple of careless mistakes. The first thought that came to my mind was that my career was ruined. Losing corporate financial data was the worst nightmare a CIO could have.

Judging from the severity of the incident, I had two options. I could resign from my company and declare that I failed my responsibilities. However, resigning was an irresponsible act. So, I was left with only one option. I needed to turn this crisis into an opportunity by telling my boss "a cup half full" story. I needed to rescue the situation and communicate with my boss to win his trust back.

I took a few steps immediately. I asked my staff member to contact a data security firm in the US to try to recover the destroyed data from the computer hard disk. I called my boss and told him that the situation was under control and that we were using all possible ways to recover the data. This included collecting information from old emails and from employee PCs of the finance team. I also took a chance. I did not shorten my family vacation because of this stressful event.

Two days later, when I returned to my office from my vacation, I had a plan to communicate. My plan was to avoid talking about how mistakes were committed. Instead, I used the opportunity to convince my boss that our data platform was highly secure, our recovery was swift and thorough, and the team behaved professionally while learning from their mistakes.

Living through this process was painful. Fortunately, the outcome was favorable as my boss was able to see my capabilities.

5.8 Strike a Balance

Telling the bad news immediately versus later

No leader likes surprises. Hence, communicating and resolving an unexpected crisis takes a lot of experience and expert knowledge.

Would you inform your bosses about a problem immediately, only to risk the possibility of being punished?

Or, would you try to fix the problem without informing your bosses, in hopes that the problem will go away without your bosses even knowing about it?

I have attempted both options for many different incidences. Although the outcome of my actions varied, telling my bosses immediately, then proceeding to fix the problem always proved to be a better option. By telling my bosses first, they may be able to offer help, it avoids potential surprises at a later stage, and most importantly, it reinforces the level of trust. Worrying about the possibility of being blamed and avoiding communication is unnecessary, and is a sign of professional immaturity.

Asking for forgiveness versus for permission

I have always believed in the saying, "It is better to beg for forgiveness than to ask for permission."

There are many situations where if we ask for permission, we receive an automatic "No" as an answer. If we are strong-willed and confident, we can push the boundaries and make things happen to our own desire, knowing that it is for the good of our career or the company. Pushing boundaries without asking for permission is not without risks and it requires good judgment.

When I worked in Ottawa, Canada as a first level manager, my company, which was a fast growing one in telecommunication research and development, was expanding its business to the United States. The company opened a branch in the Research Triangle Park (RTP) of North Carolina. Many colleagues of mine were chosen for transfer to the new facility. They were all happy to be transferred as, at the time, the United States offered more job opportunities and faster career growth than Canada. I was not identified for transfer. Eager to not miss the opportunity, I asked my manager to consider transferring me but my request was denied.

One year later, my company decided to send another group of employees to RTP. And, I found out that I was again not selected although I felt that I fully qualified for the transfer. I knew that if I asked my manager, I would be denied again. Once he denied my request, I had to live with the consequence: there would be no practical way for me to get transferred unless I defied his decision, which would never be a good idea.

Hence, I did not ask. Instead, I contacted the hiring manager in RTP and told him that I would be visiting the branch while my family and I were vacationing there. The hiring manager was happy to meet with me, as he liked my proactive approach. Of course, the "vacation" was a white lie. I paid for all my travel and hotel expenses to meet with the hiring manager. The "interview" went successfully, and he decided to offer me a job and relocate me to the United States. After I went back to Canada, I contacted the HR department and my manager regarding the job offer and the need to initiate the job transition. Understandably, my manager was not happy because I did something out of process. He told me that he could only release me to the new job after six months after completion of my project. I subsequently negotiated successfully with him to allow me to be transferred after two months. All arrangements worked out nicely.

Had I asked my manager again to transfer me, the answer would have been "No". Had I not paid for all expenses to fly to the United States to meet with the hiring manager, I would have never been able to impress him and secure the job offer. By taking this matter into my own hands, and pushing boundaries and asking for forgiveness later, I took care of my career and provided an alternative solution to our business needs.

Building Connections – Connecting with Your Boss

Summary of key points:

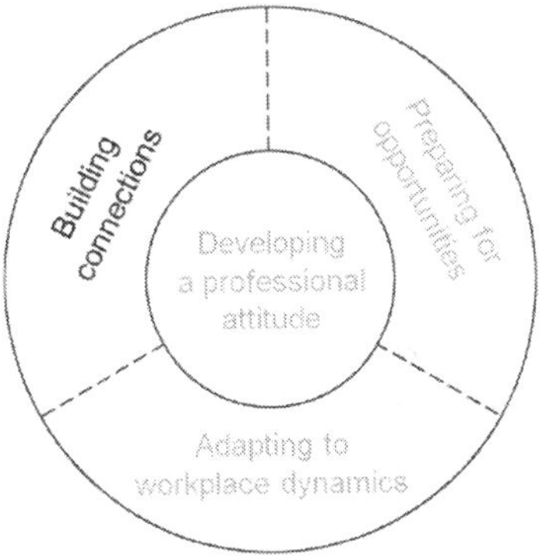
Building connections
Preparing for opportunities
Developing a professional attitude
Adapting to workplace dynamics

1. Having an all-in loyal attitude to help your boss to recover from their mistakes and to assist them to achieve business goals is important for your success. (Page 102)

2. It is important that your boss establishes the correct judgment or perception of you. Spend deliberate efforts to craft the right lens through which your boss to judge you. (Page 104)

3. Find opportunities to do something extraordinary so that your boss has something interesting to talk about you. (Page 108)

4. Follow through with doing what your boss and you have agreed. (Page 112)

5. Once you have convinced your boss to accept your idea, you have an obligation to best execute your idea and an opportunity to demonstrate your skills. (Page 114)

6. It is a rare opportunity to work for a bad boss. Use such an opportunity to improve your skills – skills that you cannot learn from a good boss. (Page 116)

7. Knowing what to learn and not to learn from a boss is important so that you avoid picking up inappropriate behaviors. (Page 119)

8. Bundle all the bad news together and tell your boss all of them at once. However, for good news, convey them one at a time in separate sequential occasions. (Page 120)

9. To build strong relationship, often, it takes persistence, sincerity, and a genuine caring heart. (Page 121)

10. There is no need to share every piece of personal information with your colleagues. When telling your personal stories and experiences, select carefully what information that you want to share, or not to share, to leave a positive professional image. (Page 123)

11. Telling your boss about a problem immediately then proceeding to fix the problem is always a better option than fixing the problem without informing your boss, in hopes that the problem will go away without your boss even knowing about it. (Page 126)

12. Take appropriate risks to push the boundary to achieve your career goals and company goals. (Page 127)

Keep your bosses and subordinates close but your peers closer.

6

Influencing Your Peers

"Who are the most difficult people to manage in the corporate workplace? Is it your bosses, your peers, or your subordinates?"

When I coach my subordinates about leadership skills, I always ask them this question.

The most difficult group is your peers – It's undoubtedly very challenging to influence and connect with them.

What is unique about your peers is that you do not have a direct organizational reporting relationship with them like you have with your bosses and subordinates. You can only influence but not dictate the actions of your peers. Peers consist of your colleagues who report to the same boss as you, people with whom you work in the same project team but do not report to your same boss, and those from another department, whom you need to influence to deliver your business goals.

Building connections with your peers is far more difficult than with your bosses and subordinates because they typically do not share the same business or personal goals as you.

6.1   Understand Your Peers' Objectives

When there are people involved, simple situations may become complex or unpredictable. I do not think there are any standard guidelines on how to establish connections with our peers. Under different situations and with different personalities, one tactic may be better than another – tactics such as treating people with respect, forging a win-win relationship, exerting positional authority, and working toward one common company goal.

However, if there exists one common attribute for a successful peer-to-peer relationship, understanding and anticipating our peers' objectives is an important first step.

I can never expect that my objectives are exactly the same as my peers even if I work for the same boss and on the same project as them. This is because every person has their personal agendas and priorities despite their work objectives. For example, my peers may prioritize spending time with their family, thus, their attitude and sense of urgency toward work may be different from mine.

Many unpleasant experiences with my peers stem from the fact that their objectives were different from mine. For example, when I was an IT director of a multinational company, a marketing director bypassed me and awarded an IT contract to a supplier without consulting me, pretending that he did not know the company policy.

Another incident happened when I was in a project team developing a telephone switching product to be sold in the United States and Japan. I was the product development manager. In order to decide whether the product passed all the criteria for manufacturing, the project team needed to take the product through a series of project gate meetings. During these meetings, decisions were made to ensure that the product met specifications and quality standards. A gate meeting decision must be supported by all key decision makers of the project team, comprising of a sales manager, a product manager, a manufacturing manager, and myself. That meant that if any one person did not support a gate decision, the introduction of the product to the marketplace would stall.

In one particular gate meeting, the team had to decide whether the product passed all the quality standards for introduction to the market. The decision was tough as there was a defect in the product. Fixing the defect before launching the product would cause a delay in schedule and a loss of anticipated market share to our competitors. During the meeting, everyone voted positively for the launch except for me, as I insisted that we must fix the defect before the product launch. My objection to launching the product created a major debate and conflict with my peers during the meeting. Especially, the sales director accused me of not understanding the company's big picture and potentially jeopardizing huge company profits and employee bonuses.

Creating conflict during the gate meeting was a mistake of mine. My mistake was that I failed to anticipate the difference in opinions of other voting members, and I brought my decision to the gate meeting as a surprise to everyone.

The conflict was caused by the fact that my objectives did not align with the other voting members' objectives. My objective was to ensure that the product was free of defect. However, the sales director's objective was to maximize sales.

I learned from this incident that before participating in a gate meeting or any decision-making meetings, it is beneficial, and sometimes necessary, to socialize my opinion with other key decision makers in a smaller group prior to the meeting. This will help me better understand other people's viewpoints.

6.2 Keep Your Peers Closer

Looking back on my career journey, I find that the more senior the position I hold, the more time I spend in building rapport with my peers.

There is a popular saying about building relationships: "Keep your friends close but your enemies closer." Peers are certainly not my "enemies". In fact, they should be my "friends". Focusing on keeping my peers closer than my bosses and subordinates has been critical to my success.

I remember when I worked as an engineer I spent more time working with my peers than working with my boss. I worked with my peers on how to design systems, solve problems, and validate solutions. In fact, every one of the companies I have worked for has emphasized teamwork.

After I was promoted to manager, my work did not require me to collaborate with peers in other groups, however I still spent a lot of time connecting with them. In fact, I spent more time building connections with my peers than with my boss. My focus on working with my peers generated ideas for continuous improvement and created better collaboration. As a result, my performance, as viewed by my boss, was always strong.

When I worked at more senior levels, it became even more important for me to keep my peers close. My focus on understanding my peers' objectives and aligning with their actions was critical for me to deliver our company goals.

There is no secret recipe of building rapport with peers. What's essential is that you spend time with them. There was one memorable conversation I had with my peer manager that proves this point.

I was a telecommunication product development manager and my team had the strongest skills in developing firmware within the company. Incidentally, a peer group needed help in firmware skills. To my surprise, the manager of my peer group did not ask me for help. Instead, he asked a team with inferior skills for help. I confronted his decision about not getting help from my team. His reason was simple and convincing. He said, "I hardly know you and your team, but I have worked with the people in the other team for a couple of projects. I have confidence in them."

Trust and confidence can only be built through working together and becoming connected. In a peer-to-peer relationship, if you are not connected, you will most likely be overlooked or by-passed.

Many years ago, my wife gave me a suggestion that has benefited my career greatly. She advised me to purposefully call at least two of my peers every week. At first, I found it very hard to follow her advice, as I did not find cold calling my peers interesting or necessary. Worse yet, I did not know how to start such a conversation. However, through practice, I gradually developed skills in initiating meaningful conversations with my peers.

Asking for help is a great way to build rapport. When asking for help from your peers, it naturally creates an environment of trust and respect. By following-through and implementing the ideas from the advice, you can further strengthen the relationship. I always believe that asking for help is a sign of strength rather than a sign of weakness. Furthermore, I perform at my best when I know when and how to ask for help.

6.3 Anticipate Surprises

The more senior of a position I hold, the more time I spend building connections with my peers. This is because I have little influence on them compared to my bosses and subordinates.

When working with my peers, I always anticipate surprises. I always assume that not every one of my peers is nice, although most of them are; they have no obligation to tell me every truth; and every peer of mine has their own priorities, which drive their behaviors. Indeed, certain people may surprise me by genuinely forgetting their commitments, deliberately skewing the facts, holding back the truth, lying, denying their promise, or worse yet, shooting me in the back.

The more senior position I hold, the more time I spend on anticipating surprises and dealing with those surprises.

6.4 Never Talk Negatively About Your Teammates

In your career, have you ever talked badly about a teammate or another employee? My advice is, don't!

In the workplace there are "bad" people whose behavior does not conform to the acceptable business and social conduct or even our own personal value system. I can think of two categories of situations where bad people may affect our emotions and normal business behaviors.

The first category is that peers working around us or with us are seemingly low performers:

- They deliver poor quality work.
- They are not team players.
- They have a poor attitude.
- They make poor business decisions.
- They are not responsive.

For this group of peers, we have to have faith that our bosses are smart enough to know the situation. The best way to deal with these poor performers is not to complain about them but focus our energy on doing our work.

Early in my career, I learned that complaining to my boss about my peers' poor performance seldom works. When I complain that my peer is not a team player, I present myself as a poor team player. When I complain that my peer has the wrong attitude, my complaint may not be viewed as the best professional attitude either.

Many of my peer leaders agree on one behavior that we cannot tolerate, that is, employees complain about their teammates' lack of competence.

The second category of situations is that people who inappropriately take advantage of their colleagues' efforts or their unique relationship with certain leaders to advance their own careers. There is no need to waste energy talking about them or finding evidence to prove their inappropriate doings.

In the business world, we are surrounded by more good than bad people. Often, the best way to deal with the bad people is to focus our energy on doing the right things for the company and avoid being unnecessarily concerned by the inappropriate behaviors of others.

6.5   Communicate to Win

One of my previous colleagues was the head of a finance team. He had many years of working experience with multinational companies and had been a financial consultant at a world-renowned business consulting firm before joining my company. I learned from him through watching how he tackled problems and communicated with his peers.

In particular, he almost always exchanged his opinions or discussed his actions with his peers in person or by phone instead of using emails. Initially, I found his behavior of deprioritizing the use of email to communicate a little bit odd and ineffective. However, as I got to learn his style better, I appreciated his emphasis on verbal and face-to-face communication.

For example, there were many times where after I sent him an email, he did not respond via email but instead he telephoned me back to discuss the matter. Sometimes, he did not get through to me by phone, so he would wait until the next morning to discuss with me in person rather than responding by email. Another behavior that differentiated him from his peers was that he almost always discussed in advance how he would tackle issues that might impact our departments. As a result, we seldom had any misunderstandings and were always clear about our intentions. Gradually, I got accustomed to his style. My connection with him and my trust in him was the best among all my peers, attributing to his assertive direct communication style.

Email is a common and popular tool for business communication. However, under the following situations, I avoid using emails.

First, I do not write and send emails when I am upset.

Without exception, emails sent when I am upset always portray the wrong tone. Consequently, recipients tend to read into my emotions and ignore the other contents of my email. Over the years, I have developed a habit in handling emails when I am emotionally disturbed by others' wrong doings: Many times when I am upset about a situation and feel the urge to write an email to express my feelings, I first write the email and hold off on sending it. I wait until the next day to read through what I have written. In nearly every situation, as I read through the email written the previous night, I find that I have over-reacted. In the end, I delete the email without sending it.

Second, I avoid using emails to debate issues or voice disagreements. Email is a powerful tool to show agreements. For example, an email that contains only two words, "I agree" conveys a strong clear positive message. On the other hand, debating a point of view is better handled using more interactive communication channels other than emails.

Last, I avoid using email when I want innovative solutions. When communicating with email, I am always cautious to convey the appropriate message and model the company's core values. Hence, in emails, I must avoid expressing my judgments prematurely and I must avoid saying things that do not align with the company vision or do not comply with company standards and policies. With the same reason, I expect my peers to use emails similarly. As a result, it is natural that if I ask my peers questions using emails, I can only get standard answers. That means that if I do not want standard answers but real or innovative advice, I talk to my peers in person.

6.6   Strike a Balance

Being the first one to communicate versus not

There are many business situations where being the first one to tell a success story, report a failure, or describe a problem is critically important. Being the first one to communicate a situation allows me to shape the situation in the right context for other people to interpret.

Telling a success story is easier than reporting a failure because successes do not come suddenly.

A success is planned and thus there is always time for us to plan ahead to determine when and how to communicate. In many cases, I draft and perfect the communication memos well before I need to send them out.

I remember once my team successfully implemented a system at fifteen different locations across the Asia Pacific region. One week before we brought the system live, I invested time to draft three communication memos, one for my subordinate to send to congratulate the project team, one for me to send to the Asia Pacific managing director and his cabinet team, and one for me to send to the global headquarters in the US to report the successful implementation.

For one whole week, I perfected the memos. I felt the effort was worthwhile as I had only one chance to communicate the success story perfectly. The memos were sent out sequentially in five-minute intervals, creating an excitement globally within the company as I had anticipated.

On the other hand, when failures and problems occur, they typically come as a surprise. Being the first one to report the problem is critical and, in some cases, the highest priority. To a certain extent it can mean disrupting other projects and sacrificing personal commitments beyond office hours.

For example, if I work in the information technology department, and if a financial system fails, it is important that I inform my boss about the system failure before the finance department does; when there is a change of government regulations about information security requirements, it is important that I report to my boss the change of requirements and a plan to tackle the change before the legal department does.

Asking for advice versus following your own innovations

Many times I have made the mistake of asking someone for help and subsequently failing to follow the advice. I have painfully discovered that this is a huge mistake. In most cases, when I fail to follow through with the advice, the person who had given me the advice loses interest to ever help me again. Consequently, I weakened my connection with the person. On the contrary, when I follow through to implement the advice, the person is more inclined to help me again in the future.

My experience has told me that one has to be smart when asking for advice:

1. If you want only a list of alternative scenarios, and not a definitive solution, you must make your intention clear when asking for help. This helps you in maintaining a strong connection with the person who gives you advice.

2. Based on the job position, some people can only provide answers that are standard guidelines and policies. If you are looking for innovative solutions or alternative approaches to address standard problems, asking may not be the right approach.

Building Connections – Influencing Your Peers

Summary of key points:

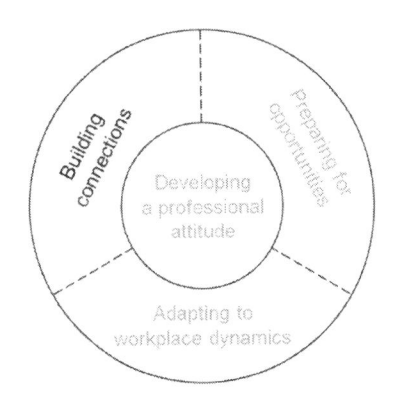

1. Understand and anticipate that your peers' objectives may be different from yours. This is an important first step to establish a successful peer-to-peer relationship. (Page 136)

2. Keep your bosses and subordinates close but your peers closer. (Page 138)

3. Asking for help is a great way to build rapport. Asking for help from your peers naturally creates an environment of trust and respect. (Page 140)

4. Anticipate surprises when working with your peers, as they have their own priorities which drive their behaviors. (Page 141)

5. Often, the best way to deal with people who exhibits inappropriate behaviors is to focus your energy on doing the right things for the company and avoid being unnecessarily concerned by others' behaviors. (Page 141)

6. To minimize misunderstanding, communicate interactively face-to-face or verbally rather than using emails. (Page 144)

7. Seize opportunities, when required, to be the first person to tell a success story, report a failure, or describe a problem, so that you are in a more proactive and controlling position. (Page 145)

8. After you have sought advice, it is important that you follow through to implement the advice. (Page 147)

Employees leave their leaders, not their company.

7

Leading Your Subordinates

"Employees continue working in a company primarily because they like their leaders and they like the work environment."

I have heard this piece of wisdom numerous times. The more experience I gain, the more I believe that leaders play a critical role in keeping good employees within a company.

7.1   Be a Leader

What is the difference between a leader and a manager?

The discussion of this question always leads to the conclusion that it is not important to explore the literal definition of leader and manager. What is important is that we understand what it takes to lead an organization, in order to achieve the best business results and to care for our employees.

I will use the word "leading" instead of "managing", since the word leading has become trendy in business conversations.

Leading an organization is not an exact science because leading involves people and no two persons share the same characteristics. That is, every employee is different because of their ethnic background, age, gender, education, work experience, professional attitude, and personal goals. And, every leader is different as reflected in their attitude and personality, and there is usually no right or wrong in their different leadership styles. For example, some leaders lead by giving clear, commanding directives on the priorities of projects and meetings, while some encourage their subordinates to act based on their self-motivation and assessment of needs; some leaders encourage their subordinates to talk to their leaders' leaders, while some do not welcome such a behavior from their subordinates.

Over the course of my career, I have collected every leadership methodology I have seen and practiced. I have grouped these leadership methodologies into a few areas:

1. Being a coach
2. Treating employees with respect
3. Developing people
4. Building and sustain a high performance team
5. Establishing an organizational culture
6. Instituting a fun work environment

In the following sections, I will talk about these leadership areas one by one and share some other general tactics that have helped me to connect with my subordinates individually and as a group.

7.2 Be a Coach

A leader can build strong connections and trust from their subordinates through coaching. Actually, many successful leaders have used the words "coach", "educator", and "teacher" to describe who they are.

In successful coaching situations, leaders invest time and treat coaching as a priority. As leaders, many already work beyond the normal business hours of their daily job, so devoting extra time to coach subordinates is sometimes a luxury. Therefore, in order to prioritize coaching employees, leaders must treat coaching as an integral part of delivering their business goals.

I purposefully dedicate time to coach my subordinates by dividing my work into three parts:

1. Work that I must do myself
2. Work that I can fully delegate to my trusted employees
3. Work items or projects that I need to teach one or two of my subordinates to get them done

I teach one or two of my staff members at a time and ultimately all staff members have their opportunity to learn from me. The following are a few examples of how I coached my subordinates.

I enjoy teaching my subordinates project management skills. I believe that these skills are best learned with on the job training from an experienced leader. Managing a project is a complex task that encompasses the management of schedules, budget, resources, and people. The skills required to lead multi-million dollar projects are no less than that required to lead a large function in a corporation. Indeed, the roles of many senior positions of large corporations are all about project management.

In one coaching arrangement, I assigned a large and critical project to a subordinate and I spent 30% of my time working with him to help him make all the decisions. I reviewed and revised his communication materials; I explained to him the dynamics of people interactions; and I helped him to navigate through complex problems.

Another coaching example is about an employee who failed to properly prioritize her work. She had two problems – she lacked good business judgments and she always delayed important actions that she did not enjoy doing. As a result, her efficiency was low. She often spent her effort working on low priority items, failing to address critical issues in a timely matter.

When I first started coaching her, I explained my observation of her problems and asked her to change. Unfortunately, her failure to properly prioritize was a result of fifteen years of inappropriate work habits. For her to change, she needed to change her mindset and attitude toward work.

For four months, I tried different tactics:
- I trained her to have a stronger business sense.
- I advised her on tools to prioritize her work.
- I asked her to drop all other tasks to spend 100% of her time focusing on only one critical action.

All these tactics gradually changed her, but slowly.

I would say that this coaching experience was not an enjoyable one for me and I felt that I failed because her speed of improvement was unsatisfactory. However, seeing her gradually improve over the long four-month period, my effort was not wasted.

Occasionally, I selectively work with my subordinates to develop their communication skills. I very much enjoyed the following working relationship with one of my subordinates.

Many years ago, my department needed to deliver a two-year project, which had eight interim milestones. The project leader I assigned was a junior one who lacked good project management and communication skills. I needed to coach him to ensure that the project would be properly delivered.

I mandated that for the first three months, he needed to review his weekly status reports with me before sending them out. For those three months, I corrected and, in many cases, rewrote his status reports. What was amazing was that after the first three months, and for the whole duration of the two-year project, he continued to ask me to review his weekly reports before he sent them out. For two years, I coached him on effective report writing skills simply because he had the internal drive to learn from me.

I often coach my employees through modeling behavior for them to imitate.

For example, I persistently demanded my subordinates to arrive at meetings on time. Based on my observation, many corporate employees have the habit of arriving late to meetings, which results in inefficiency and low productivity. In order to emphasize the importance of punctuality, I often arrive at conference rooms five minutes before meetings start.

I had one pleasant experience with a senior executive. He was a managing director of our company. He came to meetings fifteen minutes before start time. Many times, we attended the same meetings and we would be the first to arrive at the conference rooms. As a result, we both felt a strong connection.

I used to manage a team of Chinese nationals in a multinational company in Shanghai, China. English was one of many critical skills for team collaboration. Realizing my team's English deficiencies, I spent one day writing a personalized letter to each of the twenty-four selected employees to tell them where they should focus on improving their English. Each person had a different problem, for example, sounding monotone, using wrong annunciations, having low confidence, speaking too fast, and speaking too softly. My advice was to focus only on one or two of their problems and how they could improve on them. The one-day investment from me was small, but the personal connection created with the team was huge.

In order to institute the habit of following-through to my entire team, I consistently and assertively remind my subordinates that they must not rely on me to remind them about their actions once the actions were agreed between us. My reason was that they know the schedules of the agreed actions and project milestones better than I do. Typically, when I see the need and have the opportunity to remind them, the actions are already late. My assertiveness in coaching my staff on following-through has been powerful in establishing the culture of my organization.

Knowing when and how to ask for help is a personal strength, not a weakness.

Many people fail to ask for help based on a number of reasons:
- People who fail to ask for help may be introverts and asking for help may make them feel uncomfortable.
- People may wrongly assume that others are too busy to attend to their requests.
- People may be too confident and fail to see the need to ask for help.
- People may have too much pride to ask.

In my coaching sessions, I have invested a significant amount of time in encouraging my staff members to ask more questions and approach me more for help. Not surprisingly, some welcomed my idea instantly while some never changed their habits.

One tactic I often use to coach my subordinates is to ask them to write down three of their own mistakes or regrets before a coaching conversation. Mistakes and regrets are private information and they do not need to show me what they have written down. The preparation before the coaching session facilitates my subordinates to think through and prepare what they want to discuss with me. Emphasizing the need to write down mistakes or regrets works well because it forces them to think through their weaknesses, which results in more active dialogs. Not surprisingly, some staff members came up with either none or less weaknesses than I asked. Some came up with a long list, but failed to identify their biggest weakness.

Traveling with your subordinates provides the best learning experience for them.

During my career, I have had a few opportunities to travel with my mentors and senior executives for business trips. The insights I gained from their perspectives about both life and work in the casual conversations while traveling together were invaluable. As much as I could, I have reciprocated similar learning opportunities for my subordinates.

Are you a good coach?

How do you rate your own or your boss' coaching capabilities?

It's hard to gauge whether someone is good at coaching. However, someone once told me a benchmark to judge a boss. He said, "When you feel that you do not want to behave like your boss behaves, you have found a bad coach."

I am not aware of any standard benchmarks on how much time a leader should spend on coaching. Once, a human resources director gave me the following comment. "I can feel your satisfaction in seeing your employees grow and become successful. I can feel that from the way you talked about your coaching stories." Indeed, sometimes, I try extra hard to coach my employees. For example, I have treated a couple of my subordinates as apprentices. I teach them spontaneously and continuously, whenever the right coaching situation arises.

7.3 Treat Employees with Respect

When we treat people with respect, there are fewer problems created by differences in opinions, race, gender, and age. Treating employees with respect is a great way to build strong connections.

The most straightforward way to show respect to employees is to show them that we listen to their opinions. One tactic is prioritizing our response to employees' questions and emails. Whenever employees send me questions or emails, I respond immediately and take action accordingly. As a result, my employees always feel that their opinions are valued and they can feel their impact in the organization. I have found this tactic to be very successful and enjoyable.

As I respect my employees, it is natural that I pay attention to their needs.

For example, when my employees find job promotions in other departments, I support them and facilitate their job transitions. I prioritize writing reference letters to help my employees and providing performance feedback to employees as an essential part of my responsibilities.

Showing respect can be a simple, yet sincere act.

For example, I never ask my secretaries to pour me coffee. I believe that a secretary's job is not to make coffee or buy lunch for the boss. The reasons, beyond respect, are:

1. If I walk to the coffee machine to make coffee, I exercise benefiting my own health.
2. Making coffee is not good career development for secretaries.
3. Most importantly, if I do not ask my secretaries to make coffee, I treat them as an equal with personal respect.

The lower the job-rank of employees, the more I pay respect to them. I am always polite to housekeepers, drivers, and others on a lower level job than me because I believe that they could have been equally successful if they were given the opportunities to be better educated and trained. I am just more fortunate than them.

Below is one example of a small gesture that I consistently show my employees. In China, it is customary that employers give red-pockets to their employees during Chinese New Year. Red-pockets are small red paper envelopes, which contain a small amount of money that symbolize luck and fortune. It is also customary that people give less money in the red-pocket to lower rank employees. During the time I worked in China, I gave red-pockets to my employees every Chinese New Year. I gave everybody the same amount in the red-pocket, no matter what job position they held. In addition, for a few years, I deliberately gave more money to the housekeeping employees and those working in lower level jobs.

There was one incident when I failed to treat one of my subordinates with respect and it bothered me for a long time.

When I was thirty-five, I managed a fast-pace dynamic group of engineers in the US. One of my team members was fifty years old. He never joined our team for lunch and he spent the entire one-hour lunch break away from the company premises. Although he did nothing wrong he did not appear like a team player. I was not happy with the situation. As I was an immature young leader then, I made assumptions and did not communicate with this employee sufficiently to find out why he had disengaged from the rest of the team during the lunch period.

Only many years later, I found out the reason after I had a casual conversation at the company cafeteria with him. He told me how great he felt because he had been keeping fit for many years. He had skipped lunch every day and walked outdoors for 45 minutes as long as weather permitted. At that moment, I suddenly realized that I had doubted him. I should have supported his persistence in achieving his personal goals instead of doubting his intentions. I certainly had not shown him the respect he deserved when he worked for me and as a result I had failed to make a connection with him.

Respect and trust go hand-in-hand with each other.

Below is an example in which I redeemed the well-deserved respect of one of my staff members, allowing me to build a strong connection.

This example is about the situation that I mentioned previously that my subordinate accidentally committed two serious mistakes in a row, destroying all financial data along with all company data back-ups. It was a tragic disaster hurting my career and his. He was a competent employee and had a long history of delivering strong results. Due to the incident, he submitted his resignation.

My first thought was that his resignation offered me a way out. That is, he admitted the mistake and resigned. I could then pass a portion of the blame to him. However, on second thoughts, I realized it was not right to accept his resignation. I asked him to stay and told him to learn from the mistake. I asked him to find the best way to recover as much lost data as possible. I honored him with the respect that he had earned for years before the accident occurred.

A good way to show respect and trust to our employees is to honor their decisions, even if their decisions potentially lead to mistakes and we know there are better alternatives. That is, if I have the luxury to afford their mistakes, I will warn them about my prior experience and let them attempt to do it better than I have done before. I always believe that there is always more than one way to solve a business problem. Often, there is no right or wrong way. Once an approach is chosen, we deal with the outcome accordingly.

Proper delegation is essential in order to maintain trust and respect with employees. When we delegate a responsibility we also delegate the innovation of how to get the job done. Thus, when I assign tasks to my staff members, my initial position is to give them full flexibility in deciding on how to deliver the tasks. I monitor their progress and jump in to provide detailed help only when necessary.

Often, we recognize our employees of their great achievements by sending them recognition letters. A sincere email written with an appropriate level of detail of the employees' achievements goes a long way in building connections. Leaders must make these recognition emails personal and must not delegate to others the sending of these recognitions. Although it sounds odd, I have seen a few occasions when leaders asked their secretaries to send recognition emails on their behalf, potentially leading to a wrong impression that the recognitions were written by their secretaries. Despite that the emails were electronically signed by the leaders, the respect shown to the employees and the impacts of the recognitions were drastically reduced.

7.4   Develop People

It is nearly impossible for leaders to have the time and energy to develop every employee within an organization.

Picking the most competent employees to nourish has worked well for me. Only on rare occasions, do I develop low performers.

The reason for spending our limited energy on developing the most competent employees is obvious. I would like the most competent employees to stay with the company and me. In a competitive corporate workplace, it is natural that competent employees are more qualified for external opportunities and are more attracted to external recruiters. If we do not give the best opportunities to the best employees and let them know what could be next in their career, they will leave the organization. And incompetent employees will stay as they cannot afford to move, leaving a non-productive work team behind.

When I develop my best people, I focus on both their strengths and weaknesses. I often focus on only one area of strength and only one area of weakness during a given period of time.

Some people have developed a leadership charisma due to the way they were raised. I have seen many of my subordinates, including administrative support personnel, who possess qualities for promotion to higher leadership positions within the organization. Whenever I spot these people, I give them special attention and opportunities to showcase their talent.

There have been a few cases where I misjudged my subordinates' capabilities.

In one case, my subordinate had a strong personality and demonstrated a good command of leading projects. Seeing her capability, I gave her broader responsibilities and added more people to her team. However, with more staff reporting to her, she struggled in leading her team, and her subordinates gradually lost their respect of her.

Seeing what had happened but still convinced that she possessed a charisma to potentially become a senior executive, I let her lead another team, which only reinforced the fact that she was not ready. Although I was proven wrong about her leadership capability, I was not discouraged. I knew that focusing my energy to single out great people and develop them would make my job more rewarding. I misjudged people's capabilities from time to time, but through my persistent efforts I have given many people opportunities to demonstrate their strengths.

In managing the organization, it's important to sustain a good supply of career advancement opportunities to develop our employees. I have used two methods – both are practical and impactful:

1. I hire less people than I need. Fifteen years ago, I had an opportunity to listen to a keynote speech by Bill Gates, co-founder of Microsoft Corporation. One of his recommendations stuck in my mind. He said, "Once a staffing plan is established, hire one less person." The reason is that in a leaner organization, there is a need for employees to work harder and there are more career development and advancement opportunities.

2. I encourage my employees to expand their knowledge and experience from other groups or departments to broaden their vision and skills. When employees grow beyond my group's work demands, it is time to move them laterally to other departments to further grow their skills. Moving employees to other functions is a great way to broaden the skills of competent people. Often, these people get better career opportunities as they have wider and deeper perspectives of how the company works through learning from different jobs. They either move back to the original function with a higher responsibility or they advance their career quickly in the other functions.

An HR leader once asked me if it would be a problem if all my best people received training to develop their skills, which would increase their chances of being attracted to external job opportunities. My answer was simple, "I develop my best people to be better so that they are strong and are equipped to work elsewhere. However, they also have a strong desire to stay because they enjoy working in my organization and enjoy being surrounded with strong competent colleagues."

7.5 Build and Sustain a High Performance Team

In order to have a high performance team, we must equip a team with strong competent people. Competent employees like to affiliate and work with other competent employees. A high performance team is a good foundation to attract and retain competent employees, reducing employee turnover.

I always personally interview candidates for key positions of my organization. I make sure that every employee I hire has the right career aspiration, a career plan matching the opportunities my company has to offer, and the right attitude and personality. This effort ensures that every candidate fits in well with my organization and has a better chance of staying with the company.

I do not hire candidates who lack the desire to do their best in their jobs. My reason is that I cannot expect a high level of creativity from those who are content with a mediocre job performance.

A high performance team needs constant nurturing by developing the talents within the team, feeding it with meaningful projects, and grooming out poor performers.

Managing low performers is an integral part of building a high performance team. Since this book is not about how to manage poor performing employees, I will not go into the details of this topic. However, one point I would like to emphasize is that it is critically important to properly and promptly manage poor performers. If employees' poor performance is caused by their improper attitude or lack of passion and commitment, the performance problem, often, cannot be fixed by a job demotion. We either need to improve their attitude toward work or terminate their employment. Low-performing employees are like a bad virus attacking our body. They invade the good health of our organization unless we take action to remove them.

Below is an example of how I built a great team in China. I transformed a low-performing IT team that did day-to-day low level transactional work to a team of highly skilled professionals responsible for strategic business integrations, while reducing the total costs of the operations. Along with the transformation, the team grew from having limited project management skills to a team able to lead selective projects on a global basis.

In 2006, I took an assignment as the CIO of Asia Pacific of a global company in Shanghai, China. The company was not well-known in Asia Pacific, thus it was difficult to attract and retain people in the company. The team I inherited had members working in twelve different locations across six countries: Australia, China, India, Japan, Korea, and Thailand.

During the first month of my assignment, I noticed a few problems with the team. I found that:

- Over 70% of the team members did not have the right qualifications for their jobs.
- The team members located in the six countries made decisions with little reference to standards, operated independently, and seldom communicated with one another.
- The team had little knowledge of the business and limited interactions with the business.
- The team was treated as a cost liability rather than a team of strategic value to the business.

Seeing these problems, I immediately embarked on a mission to transform the team.

My first task was to hire top leaders who would work and stay with me and my company for the next four to five years. With this mission in mind, I took a three-hour plane trip to another city to see a previous colleague of mine and convinced him to join me on my journey. Paying him a personal visit was essential for two reasons. First, I needed him to be confident about his journey with me if he decided to take on the job. Second, it was important for me to see his reaction to gauge if he was the right person for the job. More importantly, I wanted him to feel his importance and my respect for him. He was not the most skilled person I knew at the time, but he was the best fit for the job and he could grow with the company. Furthermore, he had the right attitude and was a person with loyalty and high integrity. After he was onboard, I asked him to hire the strongest technical person he could find to be responsible for improving the company's information network. He quickly did that.

My next step was to transform the organization into a structure that mandates team communication and collaboration.

Since the whole organization supported the Asia Pacific region, I restructured the team to create four new regional leader positions, each with a distinct region-wide responsibility. These regional leaders had the responsibility to ensure that IT system solutions and services were implemented consistently across the region.

For each country within the region, I mandated the IT leader resident in the country to develop a strong understanding of government regulations, policies, and technology trends specific to the country.

Then, I created an operational guideline that governed team decision-making. I imposed a rule that for every major decision, two people were required to finalize the decision: a regional leader who made sure that solutions, services, business processes, standards, and talent development were implemented consistently across the region and an IT leader residing in the country who was knowledgeable about the country.

With this new organizational structure in place, collaboration within the team increased, as leaders were required to consult with one another to make company decisions.

To institute strong connections with business leaders from other functions, I enforced that my key IT leaders in each country become part of the business management team. I encouraged them to learn additional skills such as communication and strategic thinking. I personally coached each of them to become more business savvy. With stronger business connections, my team members gradually gained respect from the business and were invited to participate in key business discussions as an integral part of the business team.

With the proper organizational structure established, my final step was to equip the team with the right skills. I did this without increasing the total number of employees, which was a long arduous transforming process. I needed to terminate employees who were low performing or did not fit the new job requirements.

I was fortunate that during the time of transforming my team, the job market in Asia Pacific was prosperous. Therefore, turning over employees was not a major issue as the employees impacted were able to find jobs elsewhere easily. Indeed, it was more difficult to find people with the right skills than getting rid of those who were low performers or did not have the right skills for their jobs. With a deliberate effort, I removed many of the old team members and hired new people with the right skills.

As the team grew more competent with appropriate skills, I was able to attract more projects into my organization. I assigned multiple responsibilities to key members of the team to keep the team small and all team members busy and motivated. With more work and broader responsibilities, the team saw higher promotion opportunities and stayed with the team. And, not surprisingly, there were a couple of employees who failed to keep up with the work intensity, and resigned.

After three years, I was able to convert the team I had inherited into a highly competent one. For three years, I had had only two voluntary employee departures while the industry employee attrition rate for the IT industry was more than 15%.

A high performance team is typically a team of high morale. It serves as a platform which elevates the performance of each and every team member. Important meaningful projects flow into the team. These projects are essential to the development of the team members. In addition, if the leader focuses on developing high performers, the low performing people would feel isolated and leave the company. As a result, the team will evolve to become stronger every day.

7.6 Establish an Organizational Culture

An organizational culture reflects its leader's personality and attitude. It defines certain expectations of the leader, it instills a common mind-set in every employee, and it provides a framework for employees to collaborate and connect with one another.

Modeling behaviors that reinforce the company culture is an integral part of our job performance.

There is a restaurant in Shanghai I always enjoy visiting. As soon as I step into the restaurant waitresses who are polite and friendly greet me. I cannot help from noticing that every employee in the restaurant wears a simple uniform – a white shirt and black trousers. It is obvious that the uniforms are washed and ironed daily. Every employee serves their customers with courtesy and speed. From them, a strong message is sent to the customers: the restaurant cares. I credit this restaurant's strong personality to its leadership team and the culture they have built. This strong culture enables the restaurant to quickly assimilate new employees for them to fit in the work environment and to understand the job expectations, leading to a sustainable high quality.

I have tried different ways to build organizational cultures in different times of my career journey. In general, organizational cultures take time to build and persistent efforts to sustain.

I once instituted a culture of continuous improvement in my team. I asked all my team members to establish, as their individual goal, a minimum of one idea for continuous improvement every three months. This goal was hard to achieve for some employees. However, I accepted no exceptions. After one year, I raised the goal. I asked all team members to look beyond their own function and come up with ideas that would improve efficiencies of business processes that span multiple functions. Within two years, I shaped a continuous improvement culture in my team. My subordinates were proud of this culture.

Recently, I have instilled a culture of "HOPE" in my organization. HOPE is the short form for Helping Other People Excel.

The HOPE culture has been a great success despite that it took the team six months to evolve the initial conception of HOPE to its matured form. The idea was originated from my desire to improve our quality of serving our customers. At the conceptual stage, the team developed the motto HOPE, and deliberated on the behavioral changes that were required to make the HOPE culture realistic. Initially, only a few team members caught on to the idea.

Three months later, we reinforced HOPE with a couple of actions. First, we encouraged every member in the team to sign their emails with "HOPE - Helping Other People Excel" after their names. Second, we held a few discussion sessions for the team members to share with one another about their behavioral changes and how HOPE had influenced their day-to-day decisions. The following are some of the feedbacks from the team:

- Since the idea of HOPE was originated from the team but not a directive from the boss, I feel a strong ownership of living the culture.
- HOPE is not just about serving our customers. I now enjoy helping my colleagues within our team more.
- I have high satisfaction when I know that my effort helps other people excel in doing their jobs.

Six months after we instituted the HOPE culture, we had the whole team on board. Everyone was able to articulate what HOPE was all about. Everyone was proud to be part of the team. The impact on my team and the company has been significant. Indeed, HOPE is a noble pursuit which builds strong personal characters.

7.7 Institute a Fun Work Environment

The word fun in the context of "fun work environment" extends beyond its literal meaning. A fun work environment does not mean an environment where employees joke and play with one another. Also, it does not mean a relaxed environment without discipline.

A fun work environment is a disciplined workplace that provides a platform for employees to interact professionally and personally, and where employees find a strong sense of achievement both as in their personal growths and for the group. A fun work environment is a workplace that every employee enjoys every day.

The first example that immediately comes to mind is an environment that facilitates employees to maintain strong connections with their families. Of all the work teams I have led in different companies and industries, I allowed my subordinates to work flexible hours. The flexible working hours enabled my subordinates to easily coordinate their family routines around their work schedule and to attend to family emergencies. Of course, implementing flexible working hours may not be feasible for certain functions such as factory operations and functions that require immediate response to customers.

I know a pediatric dentist who owns a dental clinic in the US. He allows his front desk personnel to bring their young children to work when unexpected family events occur and there is no better alternative for them to take care of their children. This arrangement, though causes minor inefficiencies to the clinic, is a great solution for the staff to attend to their jobs and their family emergency needs simultaneously.

Here is an interesting question…

What is more important: working overtime to keep a project on schedule or spending time with your spouse who is sick at home?

My opinion on this and other similar situations is always that taking care of family is more important than work. Many times, my subordinates choose to loyally dedicate their time to work, thus, ignoring their family priorities. I then have to force subordinates to rightly prioritize family emergencies over work.

A workplace that has a strong learning culture and provides the best training opportunities is a fun place to work.

Throughout my career, I have insisted on a few principles. One of my principles is that I instill a continuous improvement mind-set and provide the best training opportunities to my subordinates. As far as developing employees is concerned, I persistently insist on three things:

1. I create the best on-the-job learning opportunities to every employee.
2. Employees are responsible for finding the appropriate training classes to attend.
3. Employees are responsible for eliminating any roadblocks that prevent them from attending classes that are already scheduled. I have almost never accepted being busy as my subordinates' reason to skip any scheduled training.

Furthermore, I have never cancelled my subordinates' training classes. For example, my belief is that cost reduction is not a good reason for cancelling any scheduled training as I can always save money in other areas to avoid the necessity of cancelling training classes to meet departmental budget constraints.

A fun working environment is built on employee interactions. The more opportunities there are for employees to interact with one another, the better the resultant teamwork.

I always eat lunch with my subordinates and I often organize team lunches. Some of these team lunches are on business expenses. I can justify these company-paid team lunches, since the cost of a team lunch is negligible compared to the impact a team lunch has on creating and sustaining a fun working environment.

I like short frequent off-site team-building events. For a small team where everyone works in the same location, I hold team-building events less frequently. On the contrary, if I have a diverse team with employees working in multiple countries, I need to have team-building events more often. I have found that employee team-building events provide a natural environment for employees to strengthen the trust and bond among them.

It is extremely important that employees feel the presence of their leaders. One of the many advantages of leaders marking their presence and making themselves accessible to their employees is that it facilitates open spontaneous dialog. More importantly, it sets up an open platform for employees to ask their leaders questions.

I have done a couple of things that effectively helped my subordinates to feel my presence. I walk around the work area and talk to my subordinates a lot. In addition, I almost always leave the door of my office open so that anyone can walk into my office and interrupt my work at any time.

7.8 Put Your Employees at the Right Post

I have talked about the composition and structure of a high performance team. I emphasized the importance of having high performers in the team as they attract other high performers. However, in a large organization, it is impractical and almost impossible that all team members are high performers.

A large organization has room for employees who simply want to earn a salary and put the rest of their energy on other priorities in life. I respect these people as they know their goals in life and they are focused on their goals. In fact, I would argue that it is healthy for a large organization to have a well-balanced proportion of ambitious people and average performers with minimal workplace ambitions. As leaders, it is important that we know our employees' strengths and career goals and place them at the right post to best use and develop their talents.

I believe that every employee is a genius in their own way. In a large organization, if everyone exhibits a professional attitude, there is space for everyone to innovate, contribute, and realize his or her dreams.

In a large organization, we need leaders, followers, strategists, doers, planners, analysts, auditors, and others; we need employees who possess specialized skills, employees who take care of the day-to-day operations, and employees who are experts in low-skill jobs; and we need diversity of cultures, genders, and generations to fuel innovations.

The key is to utilize people's strengths and allot them the right jobs for maximum team potential and business performance.

I once had a subordinate who was very much process-oriented. She demanded absolute compliance of guidelines and policies from her peers. However, she was too quick to speak her mind and was not tactful in her communication. As a result she did not collaborate well with many of her colleagues.

Knowing her strength and personality, I asked her to develop all the internal processes for the department and subsequently asked her to serve as an auditor, ensuring that everyone complied with the business processes. She did these two jobs extremely well.

I enjoy working with employees who are loyal or have a great professional attitude. These employees almost always do whatever it takes to complete their tasks and do the right things for the company. Hence, I always spend extra effort to earn their trust and develop their career by assigning them challenging and meaningful work.

7.9 Connect with Low Performers

How much do you value the employees working for you?

I have heard comments from one extreme of "People are expendable," to the other extreme of "People are our greatest assets." My belief is that for the vast majority of companies, people must be the most important asset.

Promptly correcting an employee's low performance problem is important. If not corrected, an employee's low performance will quickly evolve to become the leader's problem.

There are many reasons why employees do not perform up to expectations. Reasons may include:

- Lacking skills
- Lacking intellectual aptitude
- Having an inappropriate attitude
- Having a personality mismatch
- Being distracted by other personal priorities

Once leaders understand why employees underperform, they can develop action plans to deal with the low performance accordingly and quickly.

If an employee's low performance is caused by a poor attitude, it is nearly impossible to correct the performance. In such cases, I am ruthless and decisive and take prompt action to correct the situation. I give it one or two attempts to personally coach the employee to improve the performance.

In rare cases, these attempts are successful and as a result the employee connection becomes stronger than before. However, in the majority of cases, the result of my attempts leads to employment terminations. Below are some rare examples of my successes in turning around the attitude of my subordinates.

The first example is about a subordinate who stubbornly clung to his inappropriate ideas of how to lead projects. He was reluctant to learn newer skills. In one project, he failed to realize all the potential risks and missed project milestones.

I patiently helped him to bring the project back on track and taught him how to communicate with senior executives. However, because of his pride he learned only very little from me. Seeing his reaction and behavior, I decided to give him one more chance. I patiently explained to him that what he learned from his previous manager was wrong and there were better ways to execute projects. I also made it clear to him that the chance I gave him was an ultimatum. That is, if he continually failed to learn with a humble attitude, he would not be a good fit for the organization and his employment would be terminated.

Subsequently, he changed, but only marginally. Although, initially, I told him that he only got one chance to demonstrate his improvement, I continued to stay with him and hold his hand through projects because he had other good values as an employee. I made him realize that his fundamental problem was his attitude, which would take a long time to adjust. After three years of learning, he was recognized as a strong project manager by his peers and other leaders of the organization. Through my detail engagement with him, he and I built a deep and strong connection with each other.

Another example involves an employee who failed to see any career advancement opportunities within the group. As a result, she was not motivated to contribute her best to the organization. Her problem was that she wrongly assumed there was no promotion opportunity and she believed that doing an average job was acceptable. She did not realize that being content with an average performance would gradually lower her performance standard. An acceptable performance to her gradually became unacceptable to others. Her low performance standard showed through her attitude toward work. This was a situation that I had to deal with urgently. If I did not take action, her inappropriate work attitude would spread to other employees, negatively impacting the whole team.

I began by spending a two-hour, long meeting with her to listen to and analyze her thoughts. I found that she had been struggling with balancing her time at work and at home. She reasoned that if there was no advancement opportunity at work, she might as well spend more time at home. After I understood her thoughts, I told her that her job performance had been not acceptable and that she must improve and correct the situation immediately. I further explained to her a few important concepts.

- If she continues with her attitude, her performance will only get worse.
- Advancement opportunities are only given to the best performing person. Hence, she has to perform at her best before opportunities are presented to her.
- Opportunities are often created by management even though they do not exist initially.
- Promotions are awarded to people often because of their positive attitude.

With the above conversation, she decided to change. As expected, it took her a long time to correct her improper habits. With her attitude change, we both discovered that she had certain skills we both were unaware of before. She was creative; she was thorough in her work; and she had excellent organizational skills.

If you have employees who behave unprofessionally or have attitude problems, you must take responsibility for the problems and not transfer them out of your department until the problems are fixed. This means that you either bring up their performance or terminate their employment. Transferring them out to other departments only hurts the company in the long run.

Not every employee is trainable, especially those who do not have the right personality to do their jobs. For example, it is very difficult to train introverts, who enjoy working alone, to come out of their comfort zone to actively communicate with their peers. Certain employees are unwilling to approach their bosses and peers to ask for help no matter how hard they are pushed. And there are employees who cannot think strategically.

Being perfect is no fun. Thus, I always tolerate certain employees' weaknesses while I find ways to help them improve. However, when the ultimate action to terminate an employee is warranted, the best approach is to act decisively.

During performance review discussions with poor performers, I always aim to have short and succinct discussions, since long conversations tend to breed personal emotions that dilute and may negate the message to be delivered. I also aim to only give out one message during a performance discussion session. This guarantees that the message is clear and will not be misunderstood. By delivering only one message, I avoid the possibility of mixing good news with bad news, which sometimes leaves employees hearing what they choose to hear.

7.10 Establish Your Own Ambassadors

In order to establish my credibility within companies I have worked at and within the industry circle, I have spent extra effort helping my colleagues and subordinates. As a result, a few of them have become my ambassadors in promoting my professional and personal image.

I remember when I worked for a telecommunications company I had a goal to revitalize a team to have more modern technological skills. There was one person who had antiquated skills and was destined to retire in four years. If I terminated his job, he would have no hope in finding another job and would be forced to take an early retirement. He was hard working and had a great professional attitude. After a thorough consideration, I decided to protect his job so that he could continue to work till his normal retirement age and keep his income. As a result, I created a special four-year job catered to his special skill-set. He was thankful to me and I felt happy, as I had shown him that I cared about his welfare.

I always go the extra mile to develop my people. There were a few periods of time when I proactively sought out opportunities for my secretaries to be promoted to non-secretarial jobs. I have been successful in assigning meaningful work for them in the human resources department or the procurement department. Although finding higher level job opportunities for my secretaries created inefficiencies in my department, it was the best way to develop them and to maximize their contributions to the company.

Many times, I worked hard to help people from other functions within the company. This extra effort helped me build my professional image.

For example, when someone from another department asked me to sign and approve a policy document, I went the extra mile to help them correct their grammatical mistakes and sentence structures. I often actively helped people when I knew that they needed advice on their job and career. For those people whom I believed needed help, I did not wait for them to ask me, but proactively initiated conversations to extend my help.

Ironically, I have helped a couple of my best subordinates to find jobs outside of my company because there were no opportunities for them to grow within my company. Such scenarios were win-win situations for my subordinates and for the company.

The few examples I outlined above merely show that I care about the people working around me. Interestingly, the more I help my subordinates and co-workers, the more I enjoy my work. I help people not because I want anything in return but because of the sense of self-satisfaction. As my subordinates and colleagues gradually know me and enjoy working with me, my credibility increases and the number of my ambassadors increases. I am confident that one day if I asked some of my previous subordinates to quit their current jobs to join me again in my future ventures, they would do it without hesitation.

7.11 Communicate to Get Alignment

There are numerous effective ways to convey a message to our employees ensuring alignment on thoughts, actions, and values. The following examples come to mind immediately.

I know a senior executive whom I respect. He leads a global team of three hundred employees located in five continents. Connecting to his team effectively to align on his strategies and goals was important to him and was a difficult task to achieve. Considering the time zone differences and the geographical barrier, he uses a simple yet effective method to connect to every one of his staff.

Every week, he broadcasts to his global team a personal email, which he titles "Thoughts", of about three hundred words. He personalizes his thoughts with his opinions about the people he has met with, the achievements the team has accomplished, the latest technology he has read about, the mistakes he has committed, his successes, and his beliefs. The weekly "Thoughts" he sent has no fixed format and contents but every email contains something different and interesting. His message is impactful and everyone looks forward to reading his thoughts every week. I am sure that his way of broadcasting his thoughts weekly is equally effective for a smaller and less diverse group.

Inspiring my subordinates to discuss company goals proactively without me around is important. Without my presence, the environment becomes more comfortable and natural for them to talk freely and inject innovations. In order to create such an environment, I often deliberately leave meetings early to allow my subordinates to socialize among themselves.

For example, many a time, after I finish a business strategy discussion at an off-site meeting, I invite my subordinates to join me at a restaurant for an after-dinner drink and a continuation of the business discussion. In the midst of drinks and discussions, I leave the restaurant so that my subordinates continue the discussion without me being present.

Many years ago, a vice president of my company successfully instilled one of his personal values into his direct reports.

Our company was at the forefront of the telecommunications industry specialising in developing networking products for transmitting large volumes of digitized voice and data across the world. Being the first to deliver new products to the market place was essential to our business success. Hence, the vice president directed his team members to have a strong sense of urgency, and to strictly respect the element of time in everything they did.

He did two things to effectively align his team with his personal value about time. First, he frequently arranged meetings to start at 6:30am in the morning. This encouraged his team to start the day early. Second, during a period of two weeks, he locked the meeting room door when the meeting was supposed to start and he refused to let anyone who was late into the meeting room. After the two-week period, everyone was punctual attending his meetings.

7.12 Strike a Balance

Choosing the right leadership style

There are many different leadership styles and they range from one end of the extreme to another. For example, some leaders choose to manage their subordinates by measuring results delivered rather than tracking attendance records; some leaders choose to allow their employees to innovate and explore rather than forcing strict compliance with guidelines and policies; and some leaders choose to trust their employees in making decisions rather than micromanaging their actions and judgments.

Different leadership styles should be used to lead employees based on the different combinations of employee-business scenarios. And, there is no clear-cut rule on how to choose a leadership style. For example, the leadership style of leading a factory worker may be different from that of leading a research scientist; the leadership style that is effective in managing a department store may not work if used to lead a financial institution.

In my case, I always use different styles to lead different categories of employees. I honor my mature and loyal employees with trust; I coach my strong junior employees patiently; I empower my research teams to innovate and explore; I mandate my manufacturing teams to strictly observe safety procedures; and I dictate the product development team to strictly comply with operating procedures concerning information security.

Choosing between loyal employees versus capable ones

Would you rather have a loyal employee or one who is not loyal but more qualified for the job?

If there are no other major considerations, I would always hire a person who is loyal. I believe that the distribution of intelligence fits well into a standard deviation statistical bell curve. That is, a high percentage of people are of similar intelligence levels. This high percentage of people can do most jobs which do not require highly specialized skills. Many technical and professional skills can be trained. Thus, if I must choose between loyalty and capability in a person's attributes, I always look for people who have a stronger sense of loyalty.

Balancing the matching of personality versus technical capabilities

The impact of people's personalities on their job performance is huge.

For example, it is easy to understand that the performance of sales professionals is linked to their personalities. I often find that introverts inhibit their career growth in a job that requires proactive interaction with people. If job status is a gauge of success, many people have said that a person's attitude or personality determines how successful a person can be. In selecting a candidate for a job, a balance of the candidate's personality versus his technical skills is important.

Protecting your employees' interests versus your own

Leaders must take responsibility for all the work delivered by their subordinates. It is always a challenge when considering the balance between protecting a leader's personal interests and protecting the employee's interests. In my career, I have persistently shouldered responsibilities to protect my employees' interests and from the mistakes they commit.

Building Connections – Leading Your Subordinates

Summary of key points:

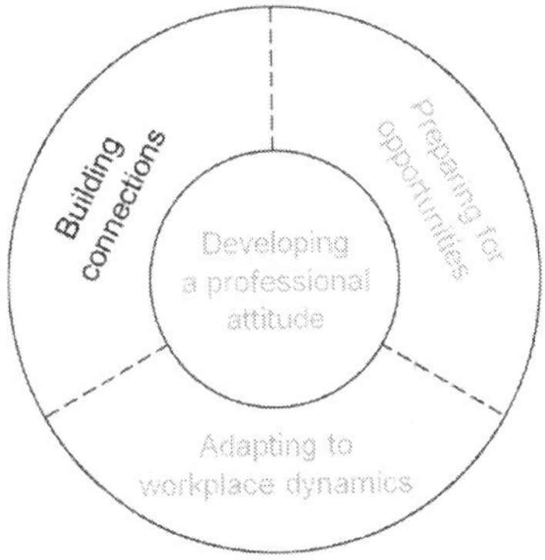
Building connections
Preparing for opportunities
Developing a professional attitude
Adapting to workplace dynamics

1. The best way to prioritize coaching employees is to treat coaching as an integral part of delivering your business goals. (Page 155)

2. Traveling with your subordinates is a good way to coach them. The insights and perspectives about work and life you share with them during casual conversations are invaluable. (Page 160)

3. When we treat people with respect, there are fewer problems created by differences in opinions, race, gender, and age. Treating employees with respect is a great way to build strong connections. (Page 161)

4. When you delegate jobs to your subordinates, you also delegate to them the innovation of how to get the jobs done, so give them the full flexibility in deciding on how to deliver the jobs. (Page 165)

5. When you spot people who possess qualities to lead at a higher level, give them special attention and the best opportunities to showcase their talent and let them know what could be next in their career. (Page 166)

6. Build a high performance team by developing the talents within it, feeding it with meaningful projects, and grooming out poor performers. Once an initial high performance team is established, it will continue to attract good people and it will evolve to become stronger every day. (Page 169)

7. Build an organizational culture that reflects your personality, defines your expectations, and instills a common framework for employees to collaborate and connect with one another. (Page 175)

8. Maintain a fun work environment that every employee enjoys. A fun work environment is a disciplined workplace that provides a platform for employees to interact professionally and personally, and that employees find a strong sense of achievement both as in their personal growths and for the group. (Page 177)

9. Every employee is a genius in their own way. Understand your employees' strengths and career goals and place them at the right posts so that they can innovate, contribute, and realize their dreams. (Page 181)

10. An employee's low performance will quickly evolve to become the leader's problem. Hence, it is important that you correct your employees' low performance decisively and promptly. (Page 183)

11. For employees who behave unprofessionally or have attitude problems, take responsibility for the problems and do not transfer them to other departments until the problems are fixed. Transferring them only hurts the company in the long run. (Page 186)

12. Spend extra efforts to develop your people and help your colleagues. As a result, they can act as your ambassadors in promoting your professional and personal image. (Page 187)

13. Use different leadership styles to lead employees based on the different combinations of employee-business scenarios. There is no one leadership style that fits all situations. (Page 192)

14. You must shoulder all responsibilities. Respectful leaders take responsibility for all the work delivered by their subordinates. (Page 194)

Stay true to your definition of success and don't be swayed by external comments or criticisms.

8

Your Search for Success

8.1 Define Your Own Success

Money and status are strong indicators of success, at least according to conventional wisdom. However, if money and status are the only two things we pursue, we will surely miss out on a lot of what is important in life.

A senior vice president of a fortune 500 company once confided his challenges to me, "Something is bothering me deeply... My company is likely to promote me to president in six months. But I know for certain that if I take the job, my wife will divorce me!" "I love my wife," he stressed.

As a senior vice president, he already had a demanding job that routinely required sixteen-hour days. For him, this meant prioritizing unforeseen work emergencies at the expense of spending time nurturing his relationship with his wife. He believed divorce was inevitable if he persisted. Despite knowing all this, his definition of success would not allow him to course correct. Six months after our conversation, his company promoted him to president, as expected, and one year after that he was divorced. He chose to give up his wife for a better career.

This senior vice president had a choice. He had plenty of money and status. Accepting the promotion would give him more of what he already had in abundance. Nevertheless, he chose to continue to climb the corporate ladder as his top priority in life.

There are many people who barely earn enough to support their family, so there is no choice but to treat work as their top priority. But if you are one of those fortunate people who can afford to choose your own path, the sooner you think about balancing your work and personal life, the more satisfying a life you will live.

I remember an interesting discussion with a friend of mine. He had a great job and had been accumulating wealth for a while. In fact, he had saved enough money to feed his family for more than 200 years! In spite of what he had achieved, he told me he would like to make even more money so that he could give a portion to his two daughters. When we had this conversation, he was already working fourteen hours a day and sacrificed a lot of his precious family time. In the end, he chose to sacrifice his time further to earn more money – money that arguably wasn't necessary for him or his daughters.

Success can only be defined when important factors such as money, job status, friends, family, community, and personal interests are all considered holistically.

One cannot win in all facets of life. You would be considered lucky and extremely successful if you were to do a good job in just two or three. In other words, success should not be narrowly defined by job status alone. You must first understand what makes you happy and what success really means to you. Only when the meaning of success is precisely defined can a corresponding career goal be established.

For example, I know many happy and successful mothers who dedicate their time to the care of family, friends, and the community. Money and status is not what really matters to them.

After working for over thirty-five years, I've come to believe that it's critical for people to maintain balance in two areas to be successful.

First, maintain balance between work and personal life.

I encourage you to think about your family and career goals in an integrated manner early in your career. If you decide to prioritize family more than your career, be proud and stay committed. Too many people in retirement wish they had spent more time with their family. That is, they would consider themselves more successful had they paid more attention to their family, even at the expense of career advancement. I firmly believe you can avoid future regret by thinking through your work-life choices earlier.

Second, stay true to your definition of success and don't be swayed by external comments or criticisms.

This balance is very hard to achieve. In the workplace and in society, we are often subject to comparisons, and it is common to judge others through the lens of wealth and job status. It is not easy to blithely ignore opinions by friends, families, and colleagues, especially if they differ from your definition of success.

Take me for example. I was raised in a humble family and was taught to be very competitive. As a result, for a long period of time, I found it very hard not to equate wealth and status with success. I was particularly sensitive to how people judged my success. For people who did not know me well, it seemed natural to me that they would judge me by my job title. It did not matter how I felt; it mattered more how other people perceived me. Hence, when it came to deciding whether to spend my time working or with my family, I unwisely chose work, although deep down I knew what was more important in the long run. Only after working hard for twenty-some years have I gradually learned to look at things differently.

"What would you like written on your tombstone?" is a question that helps many successful people reflect on what matters. With few exceptions, people are neither remembered for their wealth nor remembered for their job status. This must mean there are more important things than money, career, or other self-centered pursuits.

Does success bring happiness?

Success means different things for different people and there is no right or wrong definition. The key is to define your own success and stay true, while recognizing that your definition may evolve with each new stage of life that demands a different set of responsibilities. For me, I have learned that what define my success are family and a good heart. I've repeatedly stressed to my children that a wealthy professional is not really successful if he forgets his family or loses his way. Money can buy many things, but not a family or your character.

8.2   Follow Your Heart

If you are unhappy working at your company and you can afford to leave, follow what the inner voice of your heart tells you.

Following your heart on career decisions is not without risks. Sometimes the risks are high. Nevertheless, of all the cases I have seen and heard of people who follow their heart, the majority have resulted in a positive outcome.

I once worked in a business consulting firm in Canada. One consultant quit her high paying consulting job and moved back to Scotland, her home country, to open up a coffee shop.

Her goal was clear: she wanted to raise her children in Scotland and spend as much time as possible with them.

Her consulting job had prevented her from realizing her goal as it required frequent travel. At the same time, leaving a successful career and solely depending on her husband's income is not without risks. After much deliberation with her husband, they decided to take the leap. Her coffee shop business was slower paced as planned, and she was able to devote her time to what she felt was important. She was happy that she followed her heart. It led her to become a successful mother and entrepreneur.

A TV documentary in China followed the story of how a wine blending specialist found his calling. When in his thirties, he lived in Hong Kong and struggled to make ends meet working in unstable, low paying jobs. One day, his friend invited him to visit Xinjiang, China. They visited a few tourist attractions and were enraptured by the natural calmness and beauty of the environment. He fell in love with the surroundings and the simple life people were living. The idea of opening up a bar restaurant took root and he acted almost immediately. He quit his job in Hong Kong and transformed himself into a business owner. He successfully pursued his dream. He loved Xinjiang and built a family there, and now calls the place home.

One of my friends who had a very successful corporate career decided to switch gears in his mid-50s and devote his limited time to serve people in need. He quit his job at the peak of his career and joined a non-profit missionary to do charity work.

In 2006, when I was working in China, my company planned to transfer me back to the US after my expatriate employment contract expired. I was at a crossroad. On the one hand, I could choose to stay in China. That meant I had to quit my prestigious job, and forfeit most of my company stock awards and a generous benefit program that included a lifetime retirement pension and medical allowances. On the other hand, I could choose to move to the US with my company.

My main concern was my family.

Moving meant I would have to disrupt my children's high school education. I also knew my wife would not be happy as the city we would be transferring to was a cold place. After debating in my mind and consulting with my wife and friends for many months, I was still not able to make up my mind. I finally decided to just follow my heart. I quit my job and stayed in China. I gave up all my unvested company stock, retirement and medical benefits, and took a salary cut to join a much smaller company in a smaller role. It was a huge setback from the perspective of money and career. But I was happy and I have never regretted my decision.

In our careers, there will be many crossroads. When I am unsure which path to take, listening to my heart has invariably led me to the right choice.

8.3 Practice What You Learned

If you want to be successful, there is only one way: work hard. Once you work hard, you can work smart, which is all about delivering maximum impact to the organization and to personal priorities, given your limited time and energy. As a result, when opportunity knocks, you are more likely to be present at the right time, at the right place, and with the right people supporting you.

In this book, I have discussed various aspects of working smart, and in particular, how to form strong connections with your peers, bosses, and subordinates. Strongly connected employees foster great teamwork, since each team member will naturally be conscious of one another's goals and how to be most helpful. As a result, high performance teams emerge.

Those who are more connected in the corporate workplace will be more visible and viewed as more effective and efficient, and ultimately be given greater responsibilities.

I have devoted a few chapters on communication. Communication is an important issue and there are plenty of business books entirely dedicated to the topic. Whether you communicate to establish connections, to sell an idea, to reinforce your professional image, or to tell bad news, it is critical to think through the reason and objective of your communication beforehand and actively select the appropriate channel, structure the message, and establish the right environment for the communication.

Life is full of choices. Once a choice is made, we must live with the consequences.

In this book, I have talked about striking a balance when dealing with different situations in the corporate workplace. Often, the balance is about deciding how much time or effort to invest on an issue in the first place, as it may be time we do not have. What makes life and work interesting is that often there is no absolute right or wrong answer about where the balance should be. Where we strike the balance is often determined by our personality and life experience. As we gain more experience we also hone our intuition, and become better at tackling issues coming from the forever changing work environment.

What are the key attributes of successful people?

To mention a few:
- Diligence
- Passion
- Loyalty
- Strategy
- Commitment
- Integrity
- Execution
- The ability to follow-up

I have found that successful people do not need to possess every success attribute to be successful. In practice, it would be impossible to find people who are strong on all fronts. I believe people who are good at just two or three attributes will be able to distinguish themselves and stand out from the crowd. For me, the key attributes to my success include a positive professional attitude, loyalty to the people I work for, and keeping my commitments.

Soon after I began working, I learned the power of distinguishing myself through focusing on one key success attribute. Of all the attributes to success, I chose commitment. I wanted my colleagues and friends to think of me as a person who delivers on promises. The reason was that I observed many people, including myself, often do not follow through on promises. People often make casual promises and subsequently forget.

For example, colleagues would often say they would give an answer the next day and never did. I knew friends who promised their parents they would go home for dinner but did not follow through. I once promised a friend of mine that I would help him talk to a hiring manager about a job opening but then I genuinely forgot about it. There were times when I promised suppliers that I would give them a chance to bid on future projects and I lost track.

When I was sixteen, I beat my classmate's father in two chess games. He was so impressed with my chess skills that he promised to buy me a nice chess set. Each time we met he told me he would bring me the chess set the next time, but he never did.

There are numerous other examples where I have seen promises casually made and subsequently broken. Thinking that this was an area in which I could distinguish myself, I was determined to be serious about all my promises whether they were made formally or casually. One aspect of maturity is the ability to distinguish yourself and be different.

How much benefit my readers derive from this book will depend on your attitude, personality, and priorities in life. Indeed, if you share a similar personality and outlook to life as I do, you will identify much more with what I have written.

Attitude and personality determine how successful we become. To a large extent these are formed during a childhood. A famous quote in China states, "People's success or failure in the workplace can be traced to the kind of father they have." It is never too early to teach your children to develop the right attitude and personality.

My wife often likes to ask, "I wonder why, after living with me for over thirty years, you still have not learned how to properly handle basic housework?"

My wife and I both know the answer of course.

I do not prioritize housework. My attitude and personality do not support my putting housework into practice. I can draw the same analogy about work. There are employees who are not receptive to improving their basic skills due to their attitude and personality.

A golden rule of learning is that if one does not practice what one has learned, the knowledge will quickly be lost. With this as the final thought, I hope you will pick a couple of ideas I have talked about and put them into practice. Practice makes perfect. Practice will turn what you have learned into a habit, and habit will eventually become an inseparable part of you.

ABOUT THE AUTHOR

Dr. Addons Wu is an information services vice president and leads the digitization and information management of a predominant global business unit for Owens Corning. Addons began his career as a computer officer at a university in England. Subsequently, he held senior executive positions at Nortel Networks and General Motors, where he earned prestigious global recognitions such as Manager of the Year Award and The President's Award. During his career in China, he also served for two years as a member of the Board of Governors of the America Chamber of Commerce in Shanghai.

Addons has more than thirty-five years of experience working in five countries across three continents. He has gained substantial experience working in environments with vast cultural diversity and unique team dynamics.

ANOTHER BOOK BY THE SAME AUTHOR

Kids Come Second – And Other Unconventional Wisdom on Raising Great Children

Book reviews extracted from Amazon.com:

★★★★★ **Couldn't stop reading this book! Incredible advice and inspirational stories made it a joy to read.**

"...The author provides so much advice on inspiring your kids to succeed in life, yet he reminds us that your relationship with your spouse is and should be my #1 priority."

★★★★★ **A great book about philosophy on harmonious family and model parents, and how it positively influences kids to be successful.**

"...Overall, I like the wisdom and the life lessons from this book on establishing harmonious and balanced parent-children relationship, which is more practical and I believe it will help us to build the foundation for happy life and ground for raising successful kids."

★★★★★ **Very Instructive book.**

"...Addons can always give my son good answers by using his own experience and from the book I found many of them are more vivid and easier for parents to understand."

★★★★★ **Resolving many myths in upbringing of kids thru Addons' personal experiences.**

"...There is always a myth that once kids come to your life you have to devote more time and energy towards them and possibly your spouse become your second priority. This is not only myth but everyone thinks and behaves in the same manner. I think Addons has written beautifully how kids grow by observing their parents, and if parents together make efforts have their bonds first then certainly kids learn and become great citizens."

★★★★★ **You will learn how to make child's character begins at home.**

"...Now, my wife is reading this book to act as one entity, then we, together can encourage our children to read this book to get more motivation and right ways to go their dreams."

★★★★★ **Not a book but wisdom about how to have a happy family and brilliant children.**

"...I especially like his comments that every kid was a born genius. What parents need to do is to help them build the foundation, and the results then will naturally come."

NOTES

NOTES

Made in the USA
Charleston, SC
16 June 2014